Steps to Christ

BIBLE STUDY GUIDE

Merlin Beerman

Revelation Publications

- Compatible with any Bible
- Individuals or groups
- Contains full answer key!

ACKNOWLEDGMENT

I am grateful to our wonderful Saviour for His tremendous love, mercy, and grace. Without these gifts to us there would be no reason for this project. I thank Him for allowing me the privilege and blessing of its development.

Steps to Christ Bible Study Guide

Revelation Publications
P.O. Box 700, Tontitown, AR 72770

Editor - Carole Darmody
Illustrations - Copyright (C) Justinen Creative Group, Inc., Nampa ID
Cover Layout - Mark Decker and Merlin Beerman
Poetry - Copyright (C) Keri Ann Jenkins

Text simplified and adapted from *Steps to Christ* by E.G.White.
All Scripture references sited in the commentary are from the King James Version of the Bible.

3rd Edition
Printed in the U.S.A.

ISBN 0-9668482-0-9

TABLE OF CONTENTS

Introduction

An invitation to the reader 4

Suggestions for individual study 5

Suggestions for group study 6

Lessons

1. God's Love for Us 7
2. Our Need for Jesus 13
3. Sorrow for Sin 17
4. Admitting Our Guilt 25
5. Submission to God 29
6. Faith and Acceptance 33
7. Following Our Master 39
8. Spiritual Growth 45
9. Sharing Our Faith 53
10. Learning More About God 59
11. The Privilege of Prayer 65
12. Overcoming Doubt 73
13. Happiness in Jesus 79

Supporting Materials

Answer key 87

Certificate of Excellence 93

Inspirational material order form 95

AN INVITATION TO THE READER

We are glad you received the *Steps to Christ Bible Study Guide*. It is our prayer that you will go through these lessons and be drawn closer to the One who offers you friendship, peace, and eternal life.

If there is an address in the box below, this guide is offered to you as a gift. If you have additional questions you may write and we will prayerfully answer them for you. When you complete the course you may sign, remove, and send your *Certificate of Excellence* to this address. One of our representatives will sign and return it with additional free study materials.

On the following two pages are suggestions for individual and group study. You may use any version of the Bible to complete this series of lessons. If you want to verify your answers, or don't have access to a Bible you can find the answers in the back of this guide.

You may have been a Christian all your life, or this may be your first opportunity to learn about the wonderful love of Jesus. In either case, this time you spend in the Word of God will be a rich blessing. May the Lord fill you with peace as you seek to know Him better.

FOR MORE STUDY MATERIALS WRITE:

SUGGESTIONS FOR INDIVIDUAL STUDY

(1) **PRAY FOR GUIDANCE**

Each time you study, pray for discernment and the guidance of the Holy Spirit. Approach your study with an open mind. Avoid preconceived ideas that may have a negative influence on your search for truth.

(2) **READ THE QUESTION**

Read each question slowly taking extra time to contemplate and understand it. This will result in the greatest benefit from your study.

(3) **FIND THE ANSWER**

Use any Bible to look up the reference text listed below the answer space. Read the reference and surrounding texts to gain an understanding of their context. Write a concise answer on the blanks provided in your study guide. If you want to confirm your answer you may look it up in the answer section located in the back.

For a deeper understanding, read and compare the reference texts in multiple versions of scripture. Use a concordance, column references, and a dictionary to look up unfamiliar words and search for other related texts.

(4) **CONTEMPLATE THE RESULTS**

Reread the question and answer, then read the commentary. Contemplate the significance of what you have just studied and ask for wisdom from the Lord to help you know how to apply it to your life.

(5) **CONTINUE TO STUDY**

It is our prayer that you will continue to study God's Word. We encourage you to contact your source for this guide and obtain other inspirational materials that will aid in your spiritual growth.

SUGGESTIONS FOR GROUP STUDY

(1) ASSIGN A LEADER	It is important to appoint an individual to lead your study group. This may be a pastor, church leader, or the responsibility may be rotated among group members. The responsibilities of the group leader include: keeping the discussion objective, preventing excessive discussion on a single question, encouraging everyone to participate, and prompting the group to determine meeting arrangements.
(2) PREDETERMINE STUDY METHODS	Make a group decision whether to include outside materials in your study sessions. As a rule study time will be the most fruitful when the focus is on Biblical references.
(3) PRE-STUDY THE LESSON	Encourage each member of your group to study the lesson prior to meeting. This will result in the greatest benefit to each individual as well as enhancing his/her ability to participate in discussion.
(4) BEGIN WITH PRAYER	Each time you meet always invite the Lord to be present in your study session and the Holy Spirit to be your guide.
(5) READ QUESTION	The group leader may read or appoint another member of the group to read the questions.
(6) READ ANSWER & COMMENTARY	The group leader can ask for volunteers to give the answer and related commentary. When time allows ask for answers derived from various translations to increase participation and understanding.
(7) DISCUSSION	The most benefit will be gained if the leader does not lecture the group but rather leads them. Each member of the group should be encouraged to participate in the capacity they feel the most comfortable with. One member of the group should not dominate the discussion. Encourage sensitivity to the feelings and opinions of others even in disagreement.
(8) TESTIMONY	Have a time at the beginning or end of your session for brief testimonies. This can be general or limited to the subject matter being studied.

God's Love for Us

Lesson 1

(1) HOW DOES GOD SHOW HIS WONDERFUL LOVE?

You Give them food in due season and Satisfy the desires of every living thing

Psalms 145:15,16

In the beauty of things around us we are shown God's wonderful love. Our Father in heaven is the One who gives us life. He helps us to make good decisions, and He is the way to find joy. Look at the beautiful gifts in nature. Think of the marvelous ways He has provided for the needs and happiness of all living creatures. He has given sunshine and rain to brighten and refresh the earth. In the hills, the seas, and the plains we can clearly see our Creator's love. It is God who provides the daily needs of His creatures.

(2) IN WHAT MANNER DOES THE BIBLE DESCRIBE GOD?

God is love, and he who abides in love, abides in God

1 John 4:16

In the beginning God made man perfectly holy and happy. He created the earth with no sign of decay or death. It was the breaking of God's law, based on love, that has brought us misery and death. But even in the middle of suffering that comes from sin, God's love is very clear. Psalms 104.

In Genesis 3:17 is recorded the curse to the ground that was caused by the choice of sin and given by God for our good. The thorns and stickers are like the difficulties and trials which make our life hard. These are allowed for our good as a part of the training needed, according to God's plan, to help repair the damage that sin has caused. Even though the world has suffered the results of sin, God's love can be seen in the flowers among the thistles, and with the roses among the thorns.

"God is love" is shown on the bud of every flower that opens and on every blade of grass that grows. You can tell that God cares for us and wants to make us happy by hearing the lovely birds sing, by smelling the sweet scent of flowers in the air, and seeing the tall, beautiful trees in the forests.

(3) WHAT IS THE CHARACTER OF OUR HEAVENLY FATHER?

PARDONING INiquity
PASSING OVER THE TRANSGRESSIONS OF THE REMINATE OF HIS HERITAGE
DOESN'T RETAIN ANGER, DELIGHTS IN MERCY

Micah 7:18

In the holy Scriptures we can find out what God is like. He tells us of His unending love and mercy. When Moses prayed, "Show me Thy glory," He answered, "I will make all My goodness pass before thee." Exodus 33:18,19; Jonah 4:2.

God draws our hearts to Him by blessings which cannot be numbered. He seeks to show Himself to us through nature, and by the deepest and most tender ties that our hearts can know. But even all these fail to show the whole picture of His love.

(4) HOW DOES SATAN WANT US TO PICTURE GOD?

UNCAREING, fearful

Micah 7:17

Satan works hard to blind our minds from seeing these blessings and even though we receive them, many of us look at God in fear and think He is strict and unforgiving. Satan has deceived many into thinking that God's main goal is to punish them. He wants everyone to believe God is a severe judge who operates like a mean, merciless creditor. The devil wants us to picture our Creator as always watching closely for any mistake we may make so He can punish us. Jesus came to live here with us on earth to do away with these false beliefs and reveal the immeasurable love of God.

(5) AFTER SIN, HAS ANY MAN SEEN GOD THE FATHER?

NO ONE HATH SEE GOD AT ANY TIME --THE SON -- HATH DECLARED HIM

John 1:18

(6) HOW CAN WE KNOW WHAT THE FATHER IS LIKE?

AS THE SON REVEALS HIM.

Matthew 11:27

Jesus came down to this earth to show us His Father. When one of the disciples asked, "Show us the Father," Jesus answered, "Have I been so long time with you, and yet hast thou not known Me, Philip? He that hath seen Me hath seen the Father; and how sayest thou then, Shew us the Father?" John 14:8,9.

(7) FOR WHAT REASONS DID JESUS COME TO EARTH?

TO PREACH THE GOSPEL
HEAL THE BROKEN HEARTED
PREACH DELIVERENCE TO THE CAPTIVES
RECOVER THE SIGHT TO THE BLIND
SET AT LIBERTY THE OPPRESSED
PREACH THE ACCEPTABLE YEAR OF THE LORD

Luke 4:18

The mission of Jesus was to go around doing

good and healing those who were being attacked by Satan. There were villages where there wasn't one cry from a sick person because as He traveled through He had healed them all. The things He did revealed that He was heavenly anointed. Love, mercy, and compassion were shown in every act of His life, and His heart went out in tender sympathy to all. He became like us so that he could minister to our needs. Even the poorest and humblest people were not afraid to approach Him. Little children liked to be around Him. They loved to climb on His lap and look into His thoughtful face, gracious with love.

(8) HOW DID CHRIST PRESENT THE GOSPEL MESSAGE?

WITH GRACE AND TRUTH

John 1:14

Jesus didn't hold back one word of truth. He spoke it always in love. He was always tactful and thoughtful as He associated with people. He was never rude, never spoke a severe word or allowed pain unless it was for someone's good. He did not condemn people for their human weaknesses. He always spoke the truth in love. He exposed those who pretended to be righteous and were not. He was against unbelief and wickedness. Tears were in His voice as He warned people of their wrong-doing. He cried over Jerusalem, the city He loved, which refused to accept Him, who is the Way, the Truth and the Life. They had rejected Him, their Saviour, but He still treated them with pity and tenderness. His life was filled with unselfishness and kindness to others and every person was precious in His eyes. He showed tender respect to every member of the family of God. He saw every person as a soul who had fallen and it was His goal to save.

The character of Jesus and God, His Father, was revealed by the way Jesus lived. It is from the Father's heart that streams of heavenly compassion, which could be seen in Christ, flowed out to God's earthly children. Jesus, our tender and pitying Saviour, was God "manifest in the flesh." 1Timothy 3:16.

(9) HOW WAS JESUS TREATED ON EARTH FOR OUR SAKE?

DISPISED AND REJECTED BY MEN
MAN OF SORROWS AND AQUAINTED W/GRIEF.
HE WAS DESPISED HE BORE OUR GREIF
AND CARRIED OUR SORROW
HE WAS WONDED FOR OUR TRANSGRESSIONS
HE WAS BRUISED FOR OUR INIQUITIES
THE CHASTIZEMENT FOR OUR PEACE
WAS UPON HIM. AND BY HIS STRIPES WE ARE HEALED

Isaiah 53:3-5

Jesus came, lived, suffered and died to save us. He became a "Man of Sorrows," so we could have everlasting joy. God permitted His Son, whom He loved very much, to leave the indescribable glory of heaven and come to this world darkened with the shadow of death. He left the presence of His Father and the worship of angels, to suffer shame, insult, humiliation, hatred and death.

Look at His experience in the wilderness, in Gethsemane, and on the cross! The spotless Son of God took upon Himself the burden of sin. He who had been one with God felt in His soul the awful separation sin brings between God and man.

(10) WHAT WORDS DID JESUS CRY OUT IN AGONY?

MY GOD, MY GOD, WHY HAST THOU FORSAKEN ME?

Matthew 27:46

This suffering cry came from His lips. It was the burden of sin, the sense of its terrible effects, the separation of the soul from God that broke the heart of the Son of God.

(11) WHY DID GOD SEND HIS SON TO THIS EARTH?

that God was in Christ reconciling the world to Himself

2 Corinthians 5:19

God did not make this great sacrifice in order to create a love for us in His own heart or to become willing to save us. No, no! "God so loved the world, that He gave His only begotten Son." John 3:16. The Father doesn't love us because of this great sacrifice but He provided this great sacrifice because He loves us. Christ was the medium through which God could pour out His endless love upon a fallen world. God suffered with His Son in the agony of Gethsemane and His death on Calvary. His heart of immeasurable love paid the price so that we could be saved.

(12) HOW DID JESUS EXPLAIN THIS ACT OF LOVE?

My Father loves me because I lay down my life that I may take it again. --- This command I have received from the Father -

John 10:17,18

In other words He was saying, "My Father has loved you so much that He even loves Me more for giving My life to redeem you. In taking your place and becoming your Assurance, by giving My life to pay the price for your sins, I am dear to My Father. For by My sacrifice, God can be just, and yet the Justifier of him who believes in Jesus."

No one else but the Son of God could have redeemed fallen man because only He who was so close to the Father could have shown Him to us. Only Jesus who knew the height and depth of the love of God could fully reveal Him. There is nothing less than this infinite sacrifice made by Jesus for us that could show the Father's love to the people lost in this world.

"God so loved the world, that He gave His only begotten Son." He sent Him not only to live among us, to bear our sins, and die in our place, He gave Him to our fallen race. Christ came to identify Himself with the interests and needs of those who live on this earth.

(13) WAS JESUS ASHAMED TO BECOME ONE OF US?

He was not ashamed to call them brethern

Hebrews 2:11

He who was one with God has linked Himself with us by ties that are never to be broken. Jesus is not ashamed to call us brethren. He is our Sacrifice, our Defender, our Brother, taking our human form before the Father's throne. Through eternal ages He will be a part of the race He has redeemed. He is the Son of Man. He did all this so that we might be uplifted from the damage and shame of sin. He did it so that we might reflect the love of God, and share the joy of holiness.

(14) WHAT GREAT HONOR IS OURS?

That we should be called the children of God

1John 3:1

The immeasurable sacrifice of our heavenly Father in giving His Son to die was the price paid for saving us. This should give us greater understanding of what we may become through Christ. As John saw the great height and depth of the Father's love toward the dying race, he was filled with adoration and reverence. He could not even find the words to express the greatness and tenderness of God's love so he said, "Behold, what manner of love the Father hath bestowed upon us, that we should be called the sons of God." 1 John 3:1. What value this gives us! By sin, we come under the control of Satan, but by faith in the saving sacrifice of Jesus, we may become the children of God. By taking on human nature,

Our Need for Jesus

Lesson 2

(1) WHAT GOD GIVEN VIRTUES DID MAN LOSE BY DISOBEDIENCE?

WISDOM AND UNDERSTANDING

Psalms 111:10

Man originally had a high level of ability and a well-balanced mind. His life was perfect and in tune with God. His thoughts were pure and his aims holy, but through disobedience his powers were changed and selfishness took the place of love. His character became so weak through sin that it was impossible for him, in his own strength, to resist the power of evil. He was under the control of Satan, and would have remained so forever if God had not come to his rescue. It was Satan's goal to stop the divine plan God had in man's creation and fill the earth with grief and emptiness. Satan points to all the evil he has caused and falsely blames it on God for His work in creating man.

(2) WHY DID ADAM AND EVE HIDE FROM GOD?

BECAUSE they WERE NAKED

Genesis 3:10

When man was without sin he enjoyed a joyful closeness with God. Then after sin, he could no longer find joy in holiness, and he tried to hide from the presence of God. This is still the way it is with those who have an unrenewed heart. They are not in tune with God, and find no joy in being with Him.

(3) WHAT WILL BE THE RESPONSE OF THE UNCONVERTED TO THE PRESENCE OF CHRIST WHEN HE COMES AGAIN?

CALL for the Rocks + mountains to fall on them and hide them from God

Revelation 6:16

The sinner will not be happy in God's presence and he will try to avoid the presence of holy beings. If he were permitted to enter heaven, it would not be joyful for him. The spirit of unselfish love that rules there and causes every heart to respond to the heart of Infinite Love, would not get any response from the heart of a sinner. His thoughts, interests, and motives would be different from those of the sinless beings who live there. He would be a sour note in the melody of heaven. Heaven would be to him a place of torture; he would wish he could be hidden from Him who is light and the center of its joy. It is no accident on the part of God that keeps the wicked out of heaven. They are kept out because they are not prepared to be in the company of the righteous. The glory of God will destroy them like a fire. They will welcome destruction just so they could be hidden from the face of the One who died to redeem them.

(4) DOES ANY SINNER HAVE THE ABILITY TO CHANGE HIS OR HER OUR OWN HEART?

No

Job 14:4

It is impossible for us, by our own efforts, to escape from the pit of sin into which we are sunken. Jeremiah 13:23. Our hearts are evil and we cannot change them. "The carnal mind is enmity against God: for it is not subject to the law of God, neither indeed can be." Romans 8:7. Education, culture, will power, human effort, all have their right place, but when it comes to overcoming sin without God they are powerless. They may result in what appears to be the right behavior, but they cannot change the heart or clean the springs of life. There must be a power working from within, a new life from above before men can be changed from sinfulness to holiness. That power is Jesus. Only His grace can awaken the lifeless parts of the soul and attract it to God and to holiness.

(5) WHAT MUST HAPPEN IN OUR LIVES TO PREPARE US TO ENTER THE KINGDOM OF GOD?

BE BORN AGAIN

John 3:3

The Saviour said unless we receive a new heart that contains pure desires, renewed purposes, and new motives that lead to a new life, we "cannot see the kingdom of God." The idea that it is necessary only to improve whatever good that exists in us by nature is a deadly lie.

(6) HOW ONLY CAN SPIRITUAL MATTERS BE UNDERSTOOD?

Spiritual discernment through the Holy Spirit.

1 Corinthians 2:14

Christ said, "Marvel not that I said unto thee, Ye must be born again. The wind bloweth where it listeth, and thou hearest the sound thereof, but canst not tell whence it cometh, and whither it goeth: so is every one that is born of the Spirit." John 3:7,8.

(7) WHY DO WE CONTINUE TO STRUGGLE AFTER KNOWING WHAT RIGHTEOUSNESS IS?

WE ARE CARNAL - SOLD UNDER SIN

Romans 7:14,15

It is not enough to understand the loving-kindness of God, to see the compassion and the fatherly tenderness of His character. It is not enough to notice the wisdom and justice of His law, to see that it is built upon the endless principle of love. Knowledge alone does not bring holiness.

Paul, the apostle, expressed his struggle with this when he exclaimed, "I consent unto the law that it is good." "The law is holy, and the commandment holy, just, and good." But he added, in the bitterness of his heart-sorrow and distress, "I am carnal, sold under sin." Romans 7:16,12,14. He longed for the purity and the goodness that, in himself, he was unable to reach and he cried out, "O wretched man that I am! Who shall deliver me from this body of death?" Romans 7:24. This is the cry that has gone up to heaven from burdened hearts in all lands throughout all ages.

(8) WHO ONLY CAN DELIVER US FROM SIN, GUILT, AND DEATH?

BeHold the Lamb of God which taketh away the sin of the world

John 1:29

There is only one answer; it is thc Lamb of God. Many are the ways that the Spirit of God is used to show us the picture of this truth, to make it plain to hearts that long to be freed from the burden of guilt.

An example was when Jacob fled from his father's home weighed down with a sense of guilt for deceiving Esau. Being lonely and cast out he was separated from everything that made life dear to him. The one thought above all others that was on his mind was fear that his sin had cut him off from God; that he was forsaken by Heaven. In sadness he lay down to rest on the ground with the only things around him being the lonely hills and the heavens above filled with bright stars. As he was sleeping a strange light came into view and with it, from the plain on which he lay, a huge shadowy stairs seemed to lead upward to the very gates of heaven. Upon these stairs angels of God were climbing up and down, while from the glory above a heavenly voice was heard with a message of comfort and hope.

Jacob came to know what his heart longed for - a Saviour. He was grateful and full of joy because he was shown a way that he, a sinner, could come back to God. The mysterious ladder in his dream represented Jesus, the only means of communication between God and man. John 1:51.

(9) HOW CAN WE COME TO THE FATHER?

Through Jesus.

John 14:6

We were cut off from heaven and separated from God when man first sinned. Across the distance that lay between, there could be no communication. But earth is again in touch with heaven through Jesus. With His own merits Jesus has connected the gap caused by sin so that all of heaven can have communion with us. Christ links sinful man in his weakness and helplessness with the Source of endless power.

(10) IS THERE ANY HOPE OF MAKING IT TO HEAVEN BY OUR OWN MERITS?

NO

John 14:6

Our dreams of becoming better and improving the conditions of mankind are useless if they don't include the one Source of hope and help for the sinful race. "Every good gift and every perfect gift" is from God. James 1:17. None of us can have perfected characters unless we are connected to God who is perfect, and the only way to God is through Jesus.

(11) WHAT GREAT EFFORT FROM HEAVEN HAS BEEN GIVEN FOR OUR REDEMPTION?

THE Life of Jesus

John 10:11

The heart of God longs for His earthly children with a love stronger than death. He has poured out all of heaven in one gift. Our Saviour's coming to live and die to rescue us, the care of the angels, the pleading of the Holy Spirit, the Father working in our behalf, the unending interest of all of heaven; all these things were given for the purpose of saving us.

Think about the amazing sacrifice that has been made for us! Let us try to appreciate the effort Heaven is making to save the lost and bring them back to the Father's house. There are not any stronger reasons or more powerful methods that could be used. The special rewards for doing what is right, the joy of heaven, the companionship of the angels, the closeness and love of God and His Son, the height and extent of all our powers throughout endless ages; aren't these rewards for faithfulness good enough reasons to inspire us to love and serve our Creator and Redeemer?

In contrast to these blessings are the judgments God pronounced against sin, the shame of our character, and then final death. These are clearly presented in the Bible to warn us against serving Satan and falling for his deceptions.

Shouldn't we accept the mercy of God? What more could He do for us? Let us come to Him who has loved us with an amazing love. Let us choose the way pointed out to us so that we may be changed into His likeness. Let's welcome the fellowship of the angels that care for us and strive for a closer walk with our heavenly Father and His Son.

It is clear that without the power of Christ I cannot overcome sin and have His peace. I see my helplessness and realize my great need of Him as my Savior.

Circle: Yes No Undecided

I am thankful for God's love and the plan of redemption. It is my desire to accept this offer that He so generously gives.

Circle: Yes No Undecided

Study notes:

Sorrow for Sin

Lesson 3

(1) HOW CAN WE AS SINNERS BECOME PURE?

Repent and be Baptized

___

Acts 2:38

It is only through Jesus that we can become close to God and be made holy, but how do we come to Jesus? Many are asking the same question as the crowd on the Day of Pentecost, who, when they were convicted of sin, cried out, "What shall we do?" The first word of Peter's answer was, "Repent." Then another time, not long after, he said, "Repent, ... and be converted, that your sins may be blotted out." Acts 3:19.

To repent means to be sorry for sin and then turn away from it. We will not give up sin unless we see its wickedness; until we turn away from it with our whole heart there will be no real change in our lives.

Many of us do not understand the true meaning of repentance. Many are sorry that they have sinned and even make an outward change because they are afraid that their wrongdoing will bring punishment or suffering upon themselves. But this is not repentance in the way the Bible teaches. They cry out because of the suffering instead of the wrong they have done. This was what happened with Esau when he saw that he had lost the birthright forever.

Balaam, when he saw the angel standing in his path with a sword, admitted he was wrong so he wouldn't die; but there was no real repentance for his sin, no change of heart, no hatred of evil.

Judas Iscariot, after betraying his Lord, exclaimed, "I have sinned in that I have betrayed the innocent blood." Matthew 27:4. The confession that he had done wrong was forced from his guilty heart by an awful sense of shame and because he was scared of the punishment it would bring. The outcome that would come to him as a result of what he had done filled him with terror. In spite of this there was no deep, heart-breaking sorrow for betraying the spotless Son of God and betraying the Holy One of Israel.

Pharaoh, when suffering from the plagues of God, admitted his sin in order to escape further punishment, but returned to his defiance of heaven as soon as the plagues were stopped. All these people admitted their guilt but did not feel sorry for the sin itself.

(2) WHO CASTS OUT DARKNESS AND REVEALS THE SECRET PLACES OF THE SOUL?

JESUS

John 1:9

When the heart yields to the power of the Spirit of God it will be touched, and the sinner will see something of the depth and sacredness of God's holy law: the basis of His government in heaven and on earth. The "Light, which lighteth every man that cometh into the world," reveals the secret places of the soul, and shows the hidden things of darkness. The heart and mind become convicted of their faults. The sinner has a sense of the goodness of God. Because of his own guilt and uncleanness, he is scared to appear before the Searcher of hearts. He sees the love of God, the beauty of holiness, and the joy of purity. He longs to be clean and to be brought back to closeness with Heaven.

(3) WHAT WILL OUR PRAYER BE IF WE ARE TRULY SORRY FOR OUR SINS?

Have mercy on me Oh God
Blot out my transgressions
Wash me throughly from my transgressions
Cleanse me from my sin

Psalms 51:1-4

Create in me a clean heart
Oh God and renew a steadfast
spirit within me.

Psalms 51:10

This prayer that David prayed after his sin shows what true sorrow for sin is like. He was truly very sorry. There was no effort to cover his guilt and no desire to escape the possible punishment. David saw how great his sin was and how defiled it made his heart; he hated his sin. It was not only for forgiveness that he prayed, but for a clean heart. He longed for the joy of holiness and to be brought back into closeness with God. A confession like this is beyond our human power to do. It can come only from Jesus who has given us these gifts.

(4) WHAT IS THE RESULT OF CONFESSION?

Happyness
Blessed

Psalms 32:1,2

(5) WHAT TWO STEPS LOGICALLY PRECEDE CONFESSION?

Come to Jesus
Learn from Jesus

Matthew 11:28-30

On this very point is where many make a mistake, and as a result, they don't receive the help that Jesus wants to give them. They think that they cannot come to Christ unless they show sorrow for their sins first. It is true that being sorry does come before the forgiveness of our sins. The reason is because it is only the broken and grieving heart that will feel the need of a Saviour. But does the sinner have to wait until he has repented before he can come to Jesus? Should confession be a barrier to keep the sinner from getting to know his Saviour?

The Bible does not teach that the sinner must repent before he can accept the invitation of Christ: "Come unto Me, all ye that labor and are heavy-laden, and I will give you rest." Matthew 11:28.

(6) FROM WHAT SOURCE DOES SORROW FOR SIN COME?

Jesus

Acts 5:31

It is the goodness that goes out from Jesus that leads to true sorrow for our sins. Peter made the matter clear in his statement to the Israelites when he said, "Him hath God exalted with His right hand to be a Prince and a Saviour, for to give repentance to Israel, and forgiveness of sins." We can no more repent without the Spirit of Christ to awaken our conscience than we can be pardoned without Christ.

Christ is the source of every noble desire. He is the only One who can put hatred against sin in our hearts. Every desire for truth and purity, every realization of our own sinfulness, shows that His Spirit is moving upon our hearts.

(7) WHO DOES THE LORD DRAW TO HIMSELF?

all men

John 12:32

As we see the Lamb of God upon the cross of Calvary dying for the sins of the world, we will begin to understand the mystery of salvation. The goodness of God leads us to sorrow for our sins. In dying for sinners, Christ showed a love that we are unable to understand. As we see this love, it softens our heart and impresses upon our mind our need of a Saviour.

It is true that people sometimes become ashamed of their sinful ways and give up some of their bad habits even before they are aware that they are being drawn to Christ. But whenever they make an effort to change, with a true desire to do what is right, it is the power of Jesus that is working in their lives. A power that they don't even know is there works upon their heart. The conscience is aroused and their outward life is changed. As Christ draws them to look at His cross, to see Him whom their sins have pierced, the commandment comes home to their conscience. They can see the evil things in their life and the deepest sins of their heart. They begin to understand the goodness of Jesus and question, "What is sin, that it should cost such a sacrifice to save us? Was all this love, all this suffering, all this humiliation essential so we wouldn't perish, but have everlasting life?"

(8) WHAT IS THE WONDERFUL INVITATION JESUS HAS GIVEN?

Come, whosoever desires, let him take of the water of life freely.

Revelation 22:17

We as sinners may resist the love of Christ, but if we do not resist we will be drawn to Him. When we learn of His plan to save us, this will lead us to the foot of the cross and to sorrow for our sins which have caused Christ to suffer.

The same divine mind that is working upon the things of nature is speaking to our hearts and giving us a strong desire for something we don't have. The things of the world cannot satisfy this. The Spirit of God is begging us to seek for only those things that can give peace and rest - the grace of Christ and the joy of holiness. Our Saviour is always at work to draw our minds away from the unsatisfying pleasures of sin and attract us to the endless blessings that can be ours in Him. To all of us who are trying to drink from the broken cisterns of this world, the divine message is given, "Let him that is athirst come. And whosoever will, let him take the water of life freely." Revelation 22:17.

You who in your heart long for something better than this world offers recognize this longing as the voice of God calling to your soul. Ask Him to give you sorrow for your sins. Ask Him to reveal Jesus to you in His endless love and His perfect holiness.

(9) WHEN WE AS SINNERS SEE THE CHARACTER OF CHRIST WHAT WILL WE REALIZE?

Our righteousness is as filthy rags

Isaiah 64:6

In the Saviour's life the principles of God's law were perfectly shown as love to God and man. Kindness and unselfish love were the life of His soul. As light from our Saviour brings us understanding we begin to recognize how wicked our own hearts are.

We may praise ourselves as Nicodemus did. We may think that our life is upright and that the morals of our character are correct. We may think that we do not need to humble our hearts before God like a common sinner. But when the light from Christ shines into our soul, we see how impure we are. We see the selfish reasons for the things we do and the rebellion against God that has defiled every act of our life. It is at this point it becomes obvious to us that only the blood of Christ can cleanse us from the filth of sin and remake our heart to be like His.

It only takes one ray of the glory of God, one gleam of how pure Jesus is, getting through to our hearts to make our every wrong painfully clear. It shows the ugliness and the faults of our human character. It makes clear the unholy things that we desire, the unfaithfulness of our heart, and the unclean things we say. Our conscience is awakened and troubled under the searching power of the Holy Spirit. This awakens our great need of Christ. It becomes obvious to us that only the blood of Christ can cleanse us from the filth of sin and remake our hearts to be like His.

(10) WHAT EFFECT DID IT HAVE ON DANIEL WHEN HE REALIZED THE FLAWS IN HIS CHARACTER?

my vigor turned to fraility in me and I retained no strength

Daniel 10:8

When the prophet Daniel saw the glory of the angel that was sent to him, he realized just how weak and imperfect he was. He described this experience in the verse above. The persons who are touched in this way will hate their selfishness and their love of self. Through the goodness of Jesus they will search for the purity of heart that reflects God's law and the character of Jesus.

(11) WHAT HAPPENED TO PAUL WHEN HE SAW THE PURITY OF CHRIST, AND REALIZED THE TRUE MEANING OF THE HOLY PRINCIPLES OF GOD'S LAW?

when the commandment came, sin revived and I died.

Romans 7:9

Paul says that as "touching the righteousness which is in the law," which means as far as obeying the law was concerned, he was "blameless," but when the holy part of the law was considered, he saw himself as a sinner. Philippians 3:6. If he were judged by whether he followed the law as men see it and apply it to the outward life, he had kept from sin. Then when he realized what the real meaning of the holy principles were, and saw himself as God saw him, he bowed in shame and admitted his guilt. When he saw the holy nature of the law he saw how ugly sin really is and realized the impurity of his own character.

(12) WHAT IS THE FIRST SIN MENTIONED IN THIS VERSE, AND IS ESPECIALLY OFFENSIVE TO GOD?

Pride

Proverbs 8:13

God does not see all sin as being equal. There are different levels of guilt in His eyes. Most of us realize this also but, because of our sinful natures, our judgment is imperfect and not always fair. God recognizes all things as they really are. It is important to realize that no matter how little a wrong act may seem in the eyes of men, no sin is small in the sight of God. Revelation 20:12.

In human misjudgment the alcoholic is treated badly and is told that his sin will keep him from heaven; while pride, selfishness, and greed are often overlooked in others. These are sins that are especially insulting to God because they go against the kindness of His character and His unselfish love. When we fall into some of the greater sins we may feel a sense of shame and distress and feel a need of the grace of Jesus, but pride feels no need and keeps the heart closed to Christ.

(13) WHAT SHOULD BE OUR SINCERE PRAYER?

God, be merciful to me a sinner.

Luke 18:13

The poor Publican who prayed this prayer recognized his own sinful nature, and others looked at him the same way. The difference between him and the Pharisee was that he felt a need for forgiveness. With his load of guilt and shame he came before God asking for His mercy. His heart was open for the Spirit of God to do its gracious work and set him free from the power of sin.

The prayer of the self-righteous Pharisee showed that he felt no need for forgiveness. This reveals that his heart was not willing to listen to the Holy Spirit. Because he was so far from God he couldn't see to compare how sinful he was with the perfection and divine holiness of God. Unlike the Publican, he felt no need to change so he received nothing.

(14) CAN WE MAKE OURSELVES HOLY BY OUR OWN EFFORTS?

No

John 15:5

When we see our sinfulness, we should not wait thinking we need to make ourselves better. There are many who think they are not good enough to come to Christ. They think they should first become better through their own efforts. The truth is we have no hope of overcoming sin on our own. Jeremiah 13:23. We must not wait for a better opportunity or until we are more convinced, nor let our feelings keep us from coming to Him. We must come to Jesus just as we are and claim God's power to help us change.

(15) WHAT EFFECT DOES SIN HAVE ON A RIGHTEOUS MAN WHO LATER TURNS FROM GOD?

He shall die

Ezekiel 18:24

Some make a choice for salvation and then later, after walking in righteousness, make a choice to go back to the world. These individuals should not fool themselves into thinking that God, in His great love and mercy, will still save those who turn away from His grace.

The terrible wickedness of sin can only be realized when it is compared to what Jesus did for us on the cross. When people say that God is too good to reject the sinner, let them look to Calvary. There was no other way in which we could be saved. Without this sacrifice there was no way for us to get away from the destroying power of sin. It was because of this that Jesus took upon Himself the guilt for our sins and suffered in our place. The love, suffering and death of the Son of God all show how terrible the results of sin are. These show that there is no getting away from sin's power to destroy without the grace of Jesus. It shows that our only hope for a better life is by abiding in Him. 1 John 5:12.

(16) WHOSE EXAMPLE ARE WE TO LIVE BY?

Christ's

1 Peter 2:21

Those who reject the Lord sometimes make excuses for themselves by saying this about those who call themselves Christians: "I am as good as they are. They are no more self-denying, they don't show self-control, and they are not careful in their actions any more than I am. They love pleasure and self-indulgence as much as I do." In this way they make the faults of others an excuse for not doing what they should. But the sins and faults of others does not pardon anyone. The Lord did not give us a wrong human pattern to follow. The spotless life of the Son of God has been given for our example, and the ones who complain of the wrong choices made by those who claim to be Christians are the ones who should live better lives and set good examples. If they have such a strong belief in what a Christian should be, isn't their own sin so much greater? They know what is right, and yet refuse to do it.

(17) WHY IS IT IMPORTANT FOR US TO ALWAYS BE STRIVING TO KEEP OUR HEARTS PURE?

The Lord directs our steps.

Proverbs 16:9

Beware of putting things off. Do not put off the task of giving up your sins. With the help of Jesus, seek a clean heart. Here is where thousands and thousands have made the mistake which has led to their eternal loss. When we hold back from the pleading of God's Holy Spirit, it is sin. No matter how small a sin may seem it can be enjoyed only at the expense of tragic loss. The sins we do not overcome will overcome us and cause us to be destroyed.

Adam and Eve convinced themselves that in doing such a small thing as eating the fruit that God told them not to eat, there could not be such a terrible outcome as God had told them. But in doing this small thing they were breaking God's unchanging and holy law, and it separated all of us from God. It opened the floodgates of death and suffering upon our world. Ever since that time there has gone up from our earth a constant cry of grief, and all of creation groans and struggles together in pain as a result of disobedience. Heaven itself has felt the effects of man's turning against God. What happened at Calvary is a memorial of the amazing sacrifice that it took to atone for the breaking of the holy law. We should never think of sin as a small thing.

(18) WHAT WILL BE THE RESULT OF CHOOSING TO CHERISH KNOWN SIN IN OUR LIVES?

He is caught in the cords of his sin. He shall die for lack of instruction

Proverbs 5:22

Every time we sin, every time we don't accept the grace of Christ and turn away, it is affecting us. It is making our hearts hard, weakening our will power, and keeping us from understanding. It is making us less likely and less able to give into the tender pleading of God's Holy Spirit.

Many are quieting a troubled conscience with the thought that they can change a sinful habit when they choose to. They think they can play with the invitations of mercy, and still be impressed by the Holy Spirit again and again. They think that after turning away from the Spirit of grace and giving Satan control, in a moment of terrible need they can change their ways. They don't realize that this is not so easily done. The experiences they have had, as well as their education over their lifetime has molded their characters so well that few of them will even want to be changed into Christ's image.

Even one wrong feature in our character or one sinful desire, if cherished, will eventually do away with all the power of the gospel in our hearts. Every sinful pleasure strengthens our spirit of rebellion against God. The man who shows a boldness in not believing or a lack of interest in divine truth will reap the reward of his choices. In all the Bible there is not a more awful warning against playing with evil than the words of the wise man that the sinner "shall be holden with the cords of his sins." Proverbs 5:22.

(19) WHEN SHOULD WE RESPOND TO THE INVITATION OF SALVATION?

Now is the day of salvation

2 Corinthians 6:2

Christ is ever ready to set us free from sin, but He does not force us. If by sinning over and over our will is set on doing evil, if we do not want to be set free, if we do not accept His grace, what more can He do? We have caused our own destruction by choosing to reject His love. His invitation asks for an immediate response. Hebrews 3:7,8.

(20) WHY IS THE CLEANSING OF OUR HEART NECESSARY?

Because God sees and judges us by what is in our hearts.

1 Samuel 16:7

God knows every motive of the human heart. He knows the heart's conflicting feelings of joy, sorrow, restlessness and carelessness. He knows the heart which is the home of so much impurity and deceit. He knows its aim, its very meaning and purposes. 1 Samuel 16:7. Go to Him with your soul all stained as it is. Like David, the psalmist, open your heart to the eye of God who sees all, and say, "Search me, O God, and know my heart: try me, and know my thoughts: and see if there be any wicked way in me, and lead me in the way everlasting." Psalm 139: 23, 24.

Many people accept religion in their mind, but it is only a form of godliness when the heart is not cleansed. It should be our prayer, "Create in me a clean heart, O God; and renew a right spirit within me." Psalm 51:10. Be truthful with your own heart. Be eager and to put out as much effort as you would if your mortal life depended on it. This is a matter to be decided between God and your own heart and settled for an eternity. To believe that you will be saved without doing this will result in your loss.

(21) WHAT THINGS SHOULD WE PURSUE?

Peace with all men and holiness

Hebrews 12:14

Study God's Word in a prayerful manner. His Word shows us the very important way to be holy. These great principles are shown in the law of God and the life of Christ and without these, "no man shall see the Lord." It convicts us of sin and it clearly shows us the way to be saved. Listen and obey the voice of God speaking to your heart.

(22) WHAT RESPONSIBILITY DOES GOD ASSUME IN OUR LIVES?

reconciling us to Himself.

2 Corinthians 5:19

As you see how bad sin is and as you see yourself as you really are, do not give up in discouragement. It was sinners that Christ came to save. We do not have to win God over to us, but because of His wonderful love, God in Jesus is "reconciling the world unto Himself." He is pleading by His tender love, with the hearts of His children who have strayed away. No parent on this earth could be as patient with the faults and mistakes of their children as God is with all of us whom He is trying to save. No one could plead more tenderly with the one who has chosen to do wrong. No human lips have ever poured out a more tender offer to someone who is lost than He does. All His promises and His warnings are showing us His indescribable love.

(23) WHOM DID JESUS COME TO SAVE?

Sinners

1 Timothy 1:15

When Satan comes to tell you that you are a great sinner, look up to the One who has redeemed you and talk about His excellence. The thing that will help you is to look to His light. Admit your sin, but tell the enemy that "Christ Jesus came into the world to save sinners" and that you may be saved by His matchless love. 1 Timothy 1:15; John 3:17.

(24) WHO WILL BE THE ONES WHO WILL LOVE THE LORD THE MOST?

The Ones He has forgiven most.

Luke 7:43

Jesus asked Simon a question about two people who owed money. One owed his master a small amount, and the other owed him a very large amount, but he forgave them both. Christ asked Simon which one would love his master most. Simon answered, "He to whom he forgave most." We have been great sinners, but Christ died that we can be forgiven. The ones He has forgiven the most will love Him the most. They will stand nearest to His throne to praise Him for His great love and sacrifice that cannot be measured. The more we come to know the love of God the more we come to realize the wretchedness of sin. When we see how long the chain was that was let down for us, we start to understand about the great sacrifice that Christ has made for us, and our heart will be melted with tenderness and shame.

As I draw nearer to my Saviour I see His righteousness. I realize that my life and character are impure and unholy. It is my sincere desire to be more like Him.

Circle: Yes No Undecided

I understand that repentance is true sorrow for sin not just fear of the punishment it might bring.

Circle: Yes No Undecided

I thank Jesus for the gift of repentance He has put within my heart, and I have made the choice to act upon it.

Circle: Yes No Undecided

Admitting Our Guilt

Lesson 4

(1) SINCE OUR SINS SEPARATE US FROM GOD, WHAT DOES HE ASK US TO DO WITH THEM?

CONFESS AND FORSAKE THEM

Proverbs 28:13

The Lord does not ask us to do some painful thing so that we may have forgiveness for our sins. We don't have to make a long and tiring journey or endure horrible punishment. The conditions of receiving forgiveness and mercy from God are simple, fair, and reasonable. If we admit our sins and, with His help, turn from them we will receive mercy.

(2) WHO SHOULD WE CONFESS OUR FAULTS TO?

Micah 7:19

ONE to ANOTHER

James 5:16

First confess your faults to one another. If you have offended your friend or neighbor, you are to admit that you were wrong, and it is his duty to freely forgive you. The person you have hurt belongs to God and when you hurt him you sinned against the One who created and came to save him.

The next step is to seek forgiveness from God by confession. When we do this the case is brought before the only true Go-between, our great High Priest, who "was in all points tempted like as we are, yet without sin," and who is "touched with the feeling of our infirmities," and is able to cleanse from every sin. Hebrews 4:15.

(3) WHAT CONDITION MUST OUR HEART AND SPIRIT BE IN TO FIND TRUE PEACE?

BROKEN HEART
CONTRITE SPIRIT

Psalms 34:18

If you have not come before God with a humble heart that is broken of spirit and confessed your sins, you have not yet taken the first step in accepting peace that God offers you. If you have not gone through the admission of your guilt, hated what you have done, been sorry for doing it, and have not confessed your sins with true humiliation of your soul, you have never truly sought to be forgiven of your sins. If you have never truly sought forgiveness, you have never found the peace that only God can give. Do you have sins from your past that have not been pardoned? If so the only reason is that you have not made the choice to humble your heart and follow the conditions that God's Word gives.

(4) HOW SPECIFIC SHOULD OUR CONFESSION BE?

CONFESS SPECIFICS

Leviticus 5:5

Clear instruction is given in the Bible about this matter. Public or private confession of sin should be from the heart and freely spoken. It is not to be forced from the one who is guilty. Confession is not to be made in a light and careless way, or forced from those who don't know or realize how bad the character of sin is. The confession that is poured out of the deepest part of our soul finds its way to the God of endless pity.

True confession is always an admission of the exact wrong deed that has been done. This sin may be the kind that should be brought only before God. There may be things we have done wrong that we should confess to only the ones who have been hurt by them. Other times there may be sin that has affected a group of people. This should be confessed publicly. But all confession should be definite and to the point. We should admit the very sin of which we are guilty.

(5) WHAT SPECIFIC SIN DID THE CHILDREN OF ISRAEL CONFESS?

THEY WANTED A KING
TO BE LIKE THE OTHER
NATIONS

1 Samuel 12:19

In the days of Samuel the Israelites wandered away from God. They were suffering the results of their sin. They had lost their faith in God, lost their ability to understand His power and wisdom to rule their nation. They didn't think He was able to take care of them and defend them in what He wanted them to do. They turned away from the great Ruler of the universe and asked to be ruled in the same way as the other nations around them. But before they found peace they admitted their exact wrong: "We have added unto all our sins this evil, to ask us a king." The very sin that they were convicted of had to be confessed.

(6) WHAT MUST CONFESSION INVOLVE? (CONFESS)

MAKE OURSELVES CLEAN
CEASE TO DO EVIL.

Isaiah 1:16

Our confession will not be accepted by God unless we are truly sorry and then turn from the wrong. We must decide to change and put everything that would offend God out of our lives. This will be the result of true sorrow for sin. The part that we have to do is plainly told to us in Isaiah 1:16; 2 Corinthians 7:11.

(7) WHEN IT IS POSSIBLE, WHAT SHOULD WE DO FOR THOSE WHOM WE HAVE OFFENDED?

MAKE RESTORATION

Ezekiel 33:15

(8) WHO DID ADAM AND EVE BLAIM FOR THEIR ACTION WHICH RENDERED THEIR CONFESSION UNACCEPTABLE TO GOD?

ADAM BLAME EVE - THAT GOD GAVE HIM

Genesis 3:12

EVE BLAMED THE SERPENT.

Genesis 3:13

When sin has deadened the understanding of good, the one who is doing wrong does not notice the faults of his character and does not realize how bad the evil is that he has committed. Unless he gives in to the convicting power of the Holy Spirit he will stay in partial blindness to his sin. His confessions are not real and from the heart. Every time he admits that he has done something wrong he says he is sorry but adds an excuse about why he did it. He says that if it had not been for certain reasons he would not have done the thing he is guilty of.

After Adam and Eve had eaten of the forbidden fruit, they were filled with a feeling of shame and fear. Their first thoughts were to find an excuse so they could avoid the horrible sentence of death. When the Lord asked them about their sin, Adam answered by laying the blame partly on God and partly on Eve. The woman put the blame upon the serpent. "Why did You make the serpent? Why did You let him come into Eden?" These were the questions hidden in Eve's excuse for her sin, and by them she was blaming God and saying He caused them to fall. This spirit of self-defense was started by the father of lies and has been shown by every human who are the sons and daughters of Adam. Confessions of this kind are not brought to us by the Holy Spirit and will not be accepted by God.

(9) HOW DID THE PUBLICAN VIEW HIMSELF?

A SINNER

Luke 18:13

True repentance will lead a man to bear his own guilt for his sin and admit it without pretending to be innocent by trying to deceive. Like the poor publican, he will not even lift up his eyes to heaven and he will cry, "God be merciful to me a sinner." Those who do admit that they are guilty will be made upright, for Jesus will plead with His blood for the one who is sorry.

(10) WHAT SPECIFIC WORD USED BY PAUL IS AN INDICATION OF TRUE SORROW FOR HIS SIN?

I AM CHIEF. (SINNER)

Acts 26:10,11

In examples from God's Word where someone has shown real sorrow and shame for sin, a spirit of admitting wrong was clear. They made no excuse for their sin. One specific example is Paul. He did not try to lessen or deny his guilt as he told about his sin in its fullness. He didn't hesitate to say that "Christ Jesus came into the world to save sinners; of whom I am chief." 1 Timothy 1:15.

(11) WHAT IS A WONDERFUL PROMISE WE CAN CLAIM IF WE ARE TRULY SORRY FOR OUR SIN?

If we confess our sins
He is faithful and just to
forgive us our sins and to
1 John 1:9 cleans us from all unrighteousness

The humble and broken heart, overtaken by real sorrow for sin, will value the love of God and the cost of Calvary. As a son admits his guilt to a loving father, so will those that are truly sorry bring all their sins before God.

I see the destruction that sin has had on this world. The worst result is the separation that sin causes between God and me.

Circle: Yes No Undecided

I understand that in order to have the peace in my heart that I long for I must confess my specific sin to God and to the one I have offended.

Circle: Yes No Undecided

I praise Jesus for putting repentance in my heart. It is my choice to follow His leading and to confess and forsake my sins. I ask for His precious blood to cover the many transgressions I have committed against Him and those whom He has created.

Circle: Yes No Undecided

My prayer is that my heart will always respond to the repentance God gives to me so that I may walk in the paths of righteousness for His name's sake.

Circle: Yes No Undecided

I thank God for the victories in my life and am grateful that He has given me the promise that if I fail Him along the way I can be forgiven.

Circle: Yes No Undecided

Study notes: ______________________________

Submission to God

Lesson 5

(1) HOW SHOULD WE SEEK THE LORD?

With all our heart

Jeremiah 29:13

Our sinful nature separates us from God but the desire of His heart is that we should earnestly seek Him. It is only when the whole heart is surrendered that we can be restored into His likeness.

(2) WHAT IS OUR CONDITION WITHOUT GOD'S INTERVENTION?

Dead in tresspasses and sin

Ephesians 2:1

This verse describes the condition we are in without the Holy Spirit. God desires to heal us and to set us free from the bondage of sin. Since this requires an entire change, we must surrender everything to Him. Isaiah 1:5; 2 Timothy 2:26.

The battle we fight against self is the greatest battle that we will ever fight. The giving of ourselves by turning over all to the will of God is a struggle. Our heart must be willing to respond to God before it can be made new and holy.

(3) WHAT INVITATION GIVEN BY GOD ALLOWS OUR FREEDOM OF CHOICE?

Come let us reason together
____

Isaiah 1:18

The way God rules is not based on blind surrender. That would be control of us without reason and that is the lie Satan wants us to believe. The way God rules over us is reasonable and appeals to our conscience. "Come now, and let us reason together" is the Creator's invitation to the beings He has made. God does not force us to follow Him against our will. He cannot accept our devotion if it is not given willingly. If we were forced to obey, it would keep us from real growth of mind or character. It would make us like machines and this is not the aim of our Creator. We are the best of what He has created and He wants us to reach the greatest possible growth that we can. He offers us great blessings and wants to give them to us through His grace. He asks us to give ourselves to Him so that He may do what He knows is best for us. It is left up to us to choose to be set free from the prison of sin so we can share the glorious freedom that is given to God's children.

(4) WHAT MUST WE BE WILLING TO DO WHEN WE COME TO THE LORD?

Yor sake all that we have
____

Luke 14:33

When we give ourselves to God it is necessary for us to give up all things that would separate us from Him. Anything that draws our heart away from God must be given up. Wealth is the idol of many. The love of money and the desire for wealth is the golden chain that ties them to Satan. Fame and worldly honor are worshiped by some. The life of selfish ease and freedom from responsibility is the idol of others. These ropes that make us slaves must be broken. We cannot be half the Lord's and half the world's. We aren't God's children unless we are all His.

(5) CAN WE EARN OUR WAY TO HEAVEN?

No, By Grace, through Faith and that not of yourselves it is the Gift of God
____

Ephesians 2:8

There are those who say they are serving God, while they depend upon their own efforts to obey His law. They think they can save themselves by changing their own character. Their hearts are not moved by any deep feeling of love for Christ. They try to carry out the duties of the Christian life thinking this is what God demands of them in order to go to heaven. Religion like this is worth nothing. When Christ lives in our heart, our soul will be so filled with His love and with the joy of being close to Him that we will cling to Him. When we think of Him we will forget about ourselves, and love to Christ will be the reason for obedience. Those who feel the powerful love of God do not ask how little they may do to meet what He requires. They do not ask for the lowest standard, but try to be in perfect harmony with what their Redeemer wants them to do. With an eager desire they give their all to God. They show an interest in doing what God wants. To attempt to know Jesus without having a deep love in our heart for Him is just talk, just going through the motions.

(6) WHAT HAS CHRIST DONE SO THAT WE MAY BE SAVED?

He took upon Himself our sins.
____

Isaiah 53:6

Do you feel like it is sacrificing too much to give everything to Jesus? Ask yourself the question, "What has Jesus given for me?" The Son of God gave all; He gave His life, His love; He suffered so that we can be saved. Could it be that we, who are such unworthy objects of His great love, would withhold our hearts from Him? Every second of our lives we have been receiving the blessings of His grace. For this same reason we cannot fully realize how little we understand of the suffering from which we have been saved. Can we look at Jesus, who died for our sins, and still be willing to reject His love and great sacrifice for us?

(7) WHY SHOULD WE FEEL SORROW AND SHAME FOR OUR SINS?

HE POURE OUT His Soul unto DEATH HE WAS NUMBERED WITH THE TRANSGRESSORS, HE BORE THE SIN OF MANY. AND MADE INTERCESSION FOR THE TRANSGRESSOR

Isaiah 53:12

After seeing the immeasurable shame that the Lord went through for us, we should not grumble because we have to humble ourselves and go through struggles to enter into life.

The question that many proud hearts ask is, "Why do I need to come before God in sorrow for sin and humiliation before I can have the assurance of His favour?" I point you to Christ. He was sinless, and even more than this, He was the Prince of heaven; and in man's behalf He paid the penalty of sin for us. He was numbered with the transgressors and He bore our sins.

What do we give up, when we give ourselves to him? We give up a sinful and dirty heart, for Jesus to make pure, to cleanse by His own blood, and to save by His matchless love. And still many think this is asking too much!

(8) WHEN WE COME TO THE LORD WHAT SHOULD BE OUR GOAL IN ALL THINGS?

SEEK YE FIRST THE KINGDOM OF GOD AND ALL THESE THINGS SHALL BE ADDED UNTO YOU

Matthew 6:33

No real joy can be found by seeking the pleasures of this world. We are only hurting ourselves when we think and act against the will of God. If we choose the path of sin it will lead to suffering and death.

When we come to the Lord He does not ask us to give up anything that it is good for us to keep. In all that He does, He is always looking out for the good of His children. If all who have not chosen Jesus would realize that He has something much better to offer them than what they desire for themselves. He knows what is best for us and He plans all things for good to those who follow Him.

(9) WHAT PROMISE CAN WE CLAIM AS CHILDREN OF GOD?

I CAN DO ALL THINGS THROUGH Christ who STRENGTHENS ME

Philipians 4:19

It is a mistake to even think that God is pleased to see His children suffer. All of heaven is interested in our happiness. Our heavenly Father does not close the way of joy to any of those whom He has created. What God asks us to do is to stay away from those earthly pleasures that would bring suffering and failure, the things that will keep us from being happy and going to heaven. The world's Saviour accepts us as we are, with all our wants, flaws, and weaknesses. He will not only cleanse us from sin and rescue us by His blood, but will satisfy the desire of all who agree to wear His yoke and to carry His load. It is His goal to give peace and rest to all who come to Him for the bread of life. He asks us to do only those things that will lead our steps to the greatest joy to which those who disobey can never reach. The true, happy life of the soul is to have Jesus living in it. This is the hope of glory.

(10) HOW CAN I BECOME A CHILD OF GOD?

CHOOSE TO SERVE THE LORD

Joshua 24:15

You want to give yourself to Him, but you are weak in power to do what is right. You are slaves to doubt, and cannot get away from the habits of your life of sin. Your promises and efforts are like ropes of sand. You cannot control your thinking, your impulses, or your affections. When you recall all of your broken promises and pledges to do right it weakens your faith and makes you wonder if you ever really were sincere. This makes you feel like God cannot accept you; but don't let this depress you. What you need to understand is the true power of the will. This is the ruling power in the nature of man: the power to decide and to make your own choices. Everything depends on the right choice of the will. God has given the power of choice to you; it is yours to use. You cannot change your heart, you cannot give love to God on your own; but you can choose to serve Him. You can give Him your will and then He will help you to want to do the things He knows is best. Then your whole nature will be brought under the control of the Spirit of Christ. Your love will be centered on Him, and your thoughts will be like His.

(11) WILL ALL BE SAVED WHO DESIRE TO BE?

ONLY THOSE WHO DO THE WILL OF THE FATHER

Matthew 7:21

Desires for goodness and holiness are right as far as they go, but if you stop there they will not bring any results. Many will be lost while hoping and desiring to be Christians. They do not come to the point of giving their will to God. They do not make the choice to really be Christians.

In using the will to make right choices your whole life may be changed. By giving up your will to Christ, you connect yourself with the power that is above all kingdoms and all other powers. You will have strength from above to hold you secure, and by always surrendering to God you will be given the ability to live a new life of faith.

I see the incredible love that Christ demonstrated for me by giving His life for my transgressions.

Circle: Yes No Undecided

I am grateful that the Lord created me with freedom of choice. I gladly accept His invitation, "come now let us reason together."

Circle: Yes No Undecided

From experience I realize that the surrendering of self is the hardest thing I can do. I have come to realize the awesome sacrifice Christ has made for me. Now it is my desire to return His love by surrendering my will and dedicating my life to Him.

Circle: Yes No Undecided

Faith and Acceptance

Lesson 6

(1) CAN THERE BE PEACE AND WICKEDNESS IN THE HEART AT THE SAME TIME?

____

____

____

Isaiah 48:22

As your conscience is made more sensitive by the Holy Spirit, you begin to see the evil that sin brings. As you see its power, the guilt and the grief it brings you, a hatred for it begins to grow. You see that the sin in your heart has separated you from God and the peace He has to offer you. You see that you are a slave to the power of evil and the more you struggle to break away from it, the more you realize you are unable to. Your reasons are not pure and your heart is unclean. You see that your life has been filled with selfishness and sin. You long to be forgiven, to be cleansed, to be set free. You are asking, "How can I be close to God and become more like Him? What can I do to gain these things?" What your soul is longing for is peace.

(2) WHO IS OFFERED PEACE AND FORGIVENESS?

____

____

____

____

Isaiah 55:1

It is peace that you need - Heaven's forgiveness and love in your heart. Money cannot buy it, being wise or intelligent cannot get it for you, and there is no hope that by your own efforts you can ever earn it. But God offers it to you as a gift, "without money and without price." It is yours if you will just reach out and accept it.

(3) WHAT WONDERFUL PROMISE HAS THE LORD GIVEN US TO CLAIM IN OUR SEARCH FOR PEACE?

____

____

____

____

Ezekiel 36:26

You have admitted your sins, and in your heart put them away. You have decided to give yourself to God. Now go to Him, ask Him to wash away your sins and give you a new heart. Then believe that He has done this because He has promised. The lesson that Jesus taught while He was on this earth was that we must believe that we do receive the gift which God promises us, and if we do believe, it is ours.

(4) WHY WERE THE SIGNS AND MIRACLES OF CHRIST RECORDED IN SCRIPTURE?

____

____

____

____

____

____

____

John 20:31

Jesus healed the people of their diseases when they had faith in His power. He helped them in the things which they could see, which helped them believe and have faith in Him about the things which they could not see. He led them to believe in His power to forgive sins.

(5) WHAT IS OUR PART IN RECEIVING FORGIVENESS OF SIN?

____

____

____

____

Matthew 9:6

From this simple record of how Jesus healed the sick, we may learn something about how to believe in Him for the forgiveness of our sins. Think about the story of the paralyzed man at Bethesda. The poor sufferer was helpless. He had not used his arms or legs for thirty-eight years. Yet Jesus told him, "Rise, take up thy bed, and walk." The sick man could have said, "Lord, if Thou wilt make me whole, I will obey Thy word." But no, he didn't say this. He believed Jesus' word. He believed that he was made well, and he made the effort at once. He chose to walk, and he did walk. As he acted on the word of Christ, God gave him the power and he was made whole. Mark 11:24.

(6) CAN ANYONE BY HIS EFFORT BRING HOLINESS OF HEART?

____

____

____

Jeremiah 13:23

We are sinners who cannot make right the sins of our past. We cannot change our own hearts and make ourselves holy. But God promises to do all this for us through Jesus. We must believe His promise, admit our sins, and then give ourselves to God. We choose to follow Him and just as sure as we do this, God will do just what He says for us in His Word. If we believe the promise that we are forgiven and made clean, then God will do it. We are made whole just as Christ gave the paralyzed man power to walk when the man believed that he was healed. It is done if we believe it.

Do not wait for the feeling that you have been forgiven, but say, "I believe it and it is so, not because I feel it, but because God has promised."

(7) WHEN WE SEEK FORGIVENESS WHY CAN WE HAVE CONFIDENCE WE HAVE RECEIVED IT?

____

____

____

Matthew 7:11

There is a condition to this promise and it is that we pray according to the will of God. We know it is the will of God to cleanse us from sin, to make us His children, and to give us the power to live a holy life. So we may ask for these blessings, believe that we receive them, and thank God that we have received them. It is our privilege to go to Jesus and be made clean, and to stand before the law without shame or sorrow. "There is therefore now no condemnation to them which are in Christ Jesus, who walk not after the flesh, but after the Spirit." Romans 8:1.

(8) HOW CAN WE MAINTAIN OUR RELATIONSHIP WITH GOD?

____

____

____

Colossians 2:6

From this point on you are not your own; you have been bought with a price. "Ye were not redeemed with corruptible things, as silver and gold ... but with the precious blood of Christ, as of a lamb without blemish and without spot." 1Peter 1:18,19. By doing this simple step of believing God, the Holy Spirit has given you new life in your heart. You are born into the family of God, and He loves you as He loves His Son.

Now that you have given yourself to Jesus, do not draw back, do not take yourself away from Him, but day by day say, "I am Christ's, I have given myself to Him" and ask Him to give you His Spirit and keep you by His grace. You gave yourself to God by believing in Him and became His child. You are to continue to live in Him the same way.

(9) WHAT DOES CHRIST OFFER TO ALL WHO COME?

____

____

____

Matthew 11:28

Some seem to feel that they are always being tested and must prove to Jesus that they are changed before they can claim His blessing. But we may claim the blessing of God even now. We must have the Spirit and grace of Christ to strengthen our weaknesses or we cannot resist evil. Jesus loves to have us come to Him just as we are, sinful, helpless, and in need of Him. We may come with all our weakness, our foolishness, our sinfulness, and fall at His feet in sorrow for our sins. It is His glory to wrap His arms of love around us, to heal our wounds, and to cleanse us from all evil.

(10) WHAT REASSURANCE HAS GOD GIVEN EVERY REPENTANT SINNER?

____

____

____

____

Isaiah 44:22

This is where thousands fail because they do not believe that Jesus pardons them personally and individually. They do not take God at His word. It is the right of all who follow the conditions to know for themselves that pardon is freely given for every sin. Put away the doubt that God's promises are not meant for you. They are for every sinner who is sorry for what he has done. Strength and grace have been given through Christ and brought by ministering angels to every person who believes. No one is so sinful that he cannot find strength, purity, and righteousness in Jesus, the One who died for us. He is waiting to take away our garments, stained and polluted with sin, and put upon us the white robe of His righteousness. He is inviting us to live and not die.

(11) WHY DID GOD SEND HIS SON INTO THE WORLD?

____

____

____

____

John 3:17

God does not deal with us as worldly men deal with one another. His thoughts are thoughts of mercy, love, and of most tender concern. He says, "Let the wicked forsake his way, and the unrighteous man his thoughts: and let him return unto the Lord, and He will have mercy upon him; and to our God, for He will abundantly pardon." Isaiah 55:7. "I have no pleasure in the death of him that dieth, saith the Lord God: wherefore turn yourselves, and live ye." Ezekiel 18:32. Satan is ready to steal away the blessed promises of God. He desires to take every glimmer of hope and every ray of light from your soul but you must not let him do this. Do not listen to the tempter, but say, "Jesus has died so I can live. He loves me, and doesn't want me to be lost."

(12) HOW WILL OUR FATHER IN HEAVEN TREAT US WHEN WE COME BACK TO HIM?

____

____

____

Luke 15:20

We, just like the prodigal son, can say, "I have a kind heavenly Father. Although I have abused His love, even though the blessings He has given me have been wasted, I will get up and go to my Father, and say, 'I have sinned against heaven, and you, and am not worthy to be called Your son. Make me as one of Your hired servants.' " The story tells how the one who went astray will be welcomed.

Even this tender and touching parable does not fully show the endless compassion of our heavenly Father. The Lord has told us by His prophet, "I have loved thee with an everlasting love: therefore with loving-kindness have I drawn thee." Jeremiah 31:3. While the sinner is still far from the Father's house, wasting his money in a strange country, the Father's heart is longing over him. Every desire that comes to life in our heart to return to God is the tender pleading of His Spirit, wooing, begging, and drawing the wanderer to his Father's heart of love.

(13) WILL THE LORD EVER TURN AWAY A SINCERE HEART?

____

____

John 6:37

With the rich promises of the Bible before you, can you even question the Father's love? Can you believe that when the poor sinner longs to return, longs to quit sinning, the Lord would cruelly keep him from coming to His feet in sorrow for his sins? Do away with such thoughts! Nothing can hurt you more than to think about such a thought concerning your heavenly Father. He hates sin, but He loves the sinner, and He gave Himself to you through Jesus so that you can choose to be saved and have endless blessings in the kingdom of glory. 2 Peter 39. Is there any stronger or more tender way He could have expressed His love for you?

When you are scared and have doubts, look up to Jesus who lives to help you. Thank God for the gift of His dear Son and pray that He has not died for you in vain. The Holy Spirit is calling you today. Come with your whole heart to Jesus, and you may claim His blessing.

As you read God's promises, remember they are the way of telling us of His love and pity that cannot even be explained. His great heart of unlimited love is drawn toward the sinner with compassion that has no end. "We have redemption through His blood, the forgiveness of sins." Ephesians 1:7. Yes, believe that God is there to help you. He wants to bring back His pure image in you. As you draw near to Him by admitting and being sorry for your sins, He will come near to you with mercy and forgiveness.

(14) WILL OUR HEAVENLY FATHER EVER FORGET OR FORSAKE US?

____

____

____

Isaiah 49:15

____

____

____

Hebrews 13:5

The more time I spend with Jesus the more I realize how my sins have separated me from Him. God is giving me a hatred for sin as I see it's evil results.

Circle: Yes No Undecided

God's Word is teaching me that for my soul to be filled with peace I must seek Him with my whole heart. I realize my need to be cleansed from sins that are separating me from Him.

Circle: Yes No Undecided

I know that I cannot change my own heart nor can I remove the sins in my life. I realize that the best efforts that I make are as filthy rags. I confess my sins and ask for His strength to change.

Circle: Yes No Undecided

I believe God is just and faithful to fulfill all He promises. I believe and accept the promise that He has forgiven my sins.

Circle: Yes No Undecided

My heart is filled with peace since I have reached out to Him in faith and accepted forgiveness. I thank Him for this peace and it is my desire to continually abide in Him so that this peace will remain.

Circle: Yes No Undecided

Study notes: ________________________________

____

____

____

____

____

____

Hold On

As you lie there in darkness
surrounded with swirling thoughts,
your mind wondering
is life really worth the cost.

So many years, so much to gain,
yet so much struggle, sorrow, and pain.
My friend, these words are for you:

Hold on to your Jesus,
don't let His love go,
for He's always there for you,
He abides with every broken soul.

Hold on to His holy hand,
love Him, don't let Him go.

When all is said, when life is through,
it is He who will still be holding you.

Sweetly surrender, hold on to your Saviour,
your Jesus, your Friend.

Following Our Master

Lesson 7

(1) CAN WE TELL HOW THE HOLY SPIRIT WORKS IN OUR HEARTS?

____

____

____

John 3:8

A person may not be able to tell the exact time or place, or trace all the steps in how he was changed, but this does not mean that he isn't. The Spirit of God is like the wind. He is not seen, yet the effect is plainly seen and felt as He works upon our hearts. That renewing power that our human eyes cannot see puts a new life in the heart. He makes us new and in the image of God. Even though the work of the Spirit is silent and we don't always know He is present, His influence is working there. If the heart has been made new by the Spirit of God, that person's life will show it.

(2) HOW IS OUR LIFE CHANGED?

____

____

____

2 Corinthians 5:17

We cannot do anything to change our hearts or to bring ourselves to God. Even though we cannot and must not trust ourselves or our good works to change us, how we live will show whether the grace of God is living inside us. The way we are, our habits and the things we do will show a change. The difference will be clear about what these things have been and what they are now. The character is shown not by doing good or bad things once in a while, but by our tendencies in words and actions from day to day.

It is true that some people may act good on the outside but it doesn't come from the renewing power of Jesus. Their love of power and the desire for the respect of others may bring about a life that is in good order. Pride may be the reason some stay away from things that appear evil. A selfish heart can still do unselfish things. How can we know and determine whose side we are on?

To whom does our heart belong? Of whom do we think? About whom do we love to talk? To whom do we give our warmest affections and our best efforts? If we are Christ's our thoughts are with Him, and our sweetest thoughts are about Him. All that we have and are is given to Him. We long to be like Him, breathe His Spirit, do what He wants, and please Him in all things.

(3) WHAT CHARACTER TRAITS WILL BECOME EVIDENT IN OUR LIFE IF WE ARE TRULY BORN AGAIN?

____

____

____

____

____

____

Galations 5:22,23

Those who are truly born again no longer follow after what they used to desire. By their faith in the Son of God they will follow in His steps and reflect His character. With His power they will become cleansed and be like Jesus. The things they once hated they now love, and the things they once loved they now hate. People who were proud and bossy become humble and lowly in heart. The useless and boastful become earnest and humble. The alcoholic becomes sober, and the stained become spotless. The worthless ways and fads of the world are forgotten. Christians will not seek "outward adorning," but "the hidden man of the heart, in that which is not corruptible, even the ornament of a meek and quiet spirit."

(4) WHAT WILL WE DESIRE TO DO FOR THOSE WHOM WE HAVE WRONGED AFTER WE ARE BORN AGAIN?

____

____

____

____

Luke 19:8

There is no proof of really being sorry for our sins unless it brings changes in our lives. The Bible teaches that we should show sincere repentance by giving back what we have taken, confessing our sins, loving God and our fellow men. When we as sinners do this, we may be sure that we have passed from death and gained life. When, as sinful beings, we come to Jesus and accept His pardoning grace, love fills our heart. Every load that weights us down becomes light. The yoke that Christ wants us to carry is easy. Duty becomes a delight, and sacrifice is a pleasure. The path that before seemed to be hidden in darkness, becomes bright with beams from the Sun of Righteousness.

(5) WHAT WILL BE OUR REASON FOR LOVING JESUS?

____

____

____

1 John 4:19

The loveliness of the character of Jesus will be seen in those who follow Him. It was His joy to do what God wanted Him to do. His love to God and love for His glory, was the power that guided our Saviour's life. Love made the things He did beautiful and good. Love comes from God. The heart that is not true to God cannot create love or cause it to grow. It can only be found in someone's heart where Jesus rules. In the heart made new by the grace of Jesus, love dominates.

(6) WHAT WILL WE DESIRE TO DO TO SHOW OUR LOVE TO GOD?

____

____

____

John 14:15

Love changes us. It shows us what we should do, it gives us control over our passions, it is stronger then hatred, and helps us care for others. This love, cherished in our heart, brings us blessings as well as to those around us.

(7) WHY IS OBEDIENCE, BY THE POWER OF CHRIST, ESSENTIAL IN OUR RELATIONSHIP WITH HIM?

____

____

____

____

____

1 John 2:4

There are two kinds of mistakes that the children of God need to guard against, especially those who have just come to trust in the grace of Jesus. The first one that already has been mentioned, is to think that we can bring ourselves to God by our own works or efforts. Galations 2:16. If we try to become holy by our own works in keeping the law, we are attempting to do what is impossible. All that we do without Christ is polluted with selfishness and sin. It is only the grace of Christ that comes by faith, that can make us holy. Jeremiah 13:23.

The second danger, which is the opposite but no less dangerous, is believing that the grace of Jesus releases us from having to obey the law of God. It is dangerous to think that since by faith alone we can have the grace of Christ we can continue in the ways of the world. Our works and actions will not get us into heaven but they certainly show where our heart is.

(8) WHEN WE ARE BORN AGAIN WHAT HAS CHRIST PROMISED TO DO?

____

____

____

Hebrews 10:16

The law of God is an expression of who God is. It is a summary of the great principle of love, upon which His government in heaven and on earth is based. If our hearts are made new in the likeness of God, if God's love is present there, won't the law of God be carried out in our life? When the principle of love is living in our heart, when we are made new in the image of our Creator, the new-covenant promise becomes true: "I will put My laws into their hearts, and in their minds will I write them." And if the law is written in our heart, won't it shape our life? Obedience, the service and loyalty of love, is the true sign that we are following Jesus. Instead of freeing us from having to obey, it is faith, and faith only, that lets us take part in the grace of Jesus. Then, by grace, we are given the desire and ability to obey Him.

(9) WHAT REVEALS WHO OUR MASTER IS?

____

____

____

Matthew 7:16

We do not earn salvation by the act of obedience, it is a free gift from God that we get by faith. Obedience will result as the fruit of faith. Matthew 7:20. If we are one with Christ, if God's love lives in us, our feelings, our thoughts, our motives, and the things we do will be in tune with what God wants us to do. And to do what is right is determined by the standard of God's holy law, which is shown us in the ten principles given on Sinai. Romans 7:7; Romans 3:20; 1 John 3:8,9.

(10) WHAT TWO ELEMENTS SHOULD BE EQUALLY PRESENT IN OUR LIFE AFTER GIVING OUR HEART TO THE LORD?

___

___

James 2:17

When people think they have faith in Christ and claim it releases them from the responsibility of obeying God, this is not faith, it is presumption. "By grace are ye saved through faith." But "faith, if it hath not works, is dead." Jesus said this about Himself before He came to earth, "I delight to do Thy will, O My God: yea, Thy law is within My heart." Psalm 40:8. And just before He went back to heaven He said, "I have kept My Father's commandments, and abide in His love." John 15:10. This Scripture says, "Hereby we do know that we know Him, if we keep His commandments." 1 John 2:3.

(11) HOW DO WE KNOW HOW TO LIVE OUR LIVES?

___

___

___

1 Peter 2:21

(12) HOW CAN WE HAVE RIGHTEOUSNESS AND ETERNAL LIFE?

___

___

___

2 Corinthians 5:21

The way to live eternally is the same now as it has always been. It is just what it was in the Garden of Eden before the fall of our first parents. It is to obey the Law of God; it is perfect righteousness. If eternal life were to be allowed to any being under any other conditions the happiness of the whole universe would be at risk. The way would be open for sin to last forever with all the grief and suffering that comes with it. So what is our hope? It is to accept the sacrifice of Jesus to pay the penalty for our sin, and allow Christ's righteousness to cover us.

(13) WHAT IS OFFERED TO US BY THE BLOOD OF CHRIST THAT GIVES US THE POWER TO BE HOLY?

___

___

___

Ephesians 1:7

(14) WHAT PRIVILEGE DOES GOD OFFER EACH OF US?

___

___

___

___

2 Peter 1:4

Before Adam sinned he had a righteous character and it was his desire to obey the Law of God. But, as a result of sin, his desires changed from righteousness to evil and we have inherited this same fallen nature. Since we are sinful and unholy we cannot perfectly obey the holy law. We do not have the ability to do what is right on our own so we are unable to obey the Law of God. But Jesus has made a way of escape for us. He lived on earth and experienced the trials and temptations we go through. He lived a sinless life, then died for us, and now He offers to take our sins and give us His righteousness. If we give ourselves to Him and accept Him as our Saviour, for His sake we are counted righteous no matter how sinful our lives may have been. Christ's character stands in place of our character, and we are accepted before God just as if we had not sinned.

(15) AFTER OUR REBIRTH HOW DO WE CONTINUE TO WALK WITH OUR SAVIOUR?

____

____

____

Galatians 2:20

When we are born again Christ changes our heart. He comes in and stays in our heart by faith. We are to keep close to Jesus by faith and by continually giving our will to Him. As long as we do this, He will work in us His will and help us to do the things He wants us to do, living according to the way described in Galatians 2:20. Jesus said to His disciples, "It is not ye that speak, but the Spirit of your Father which speaketh in you." Matthew 10:20. Then with Christ working in us, we will obey God and do what is right.

We do not have any reason to try to lift ourselves up. Our only reason for hope is in the goodness of Jesus and the presence of the Holy Spirit in our lives.

(16) WHAT STATEMENT IN THIS VERSE REVEALS THAT FAITH IS DIFFERENT FROM BELIEF?

____

____

____

James 2:19

When we talk about faith and belief, there is a difference that should be kept in mind. There is a kind of belief that is totally different from faith. God exists, He is powerful and the fact that His Word is true, even Satan and the fallen angels cannot at heart deny. The Bible says that "the devils also believe, and tremble," but this is not faith. For true faith that works by love and purifies the soul, we must believe in God's Word, surrender our will and heart to Him with our affections fixed upon Him. Through this faith our heart is made new in the image of God. And the heart that has not been made new does not follow the law of God - in fact it cannot. A heart that is made new delights in the holy principles of the law by saying like David, the psalmist, "O how love I Thy law! it is my meditation all the day." Psalm 119:97. And the goodness of the law is finished in us, "who walk not after the flesh, but after the Spirit." Romans 8:1.

(17) HOW LONG WILL CHRIST CONTINUE TO PATIENTLY REFINE OUR CHARACTERS?

____

____

____

____

1 John 2:1

You may have known the forgiving love of Jesus and really want to be a child of God. You realize that your character is imperfect, your life has many things wrong with it. You may have doubts about whether your heart has really been made new by the Holy Spirit. If this is what you are feeling do not be discouraged. Many times we will have to bow down and weep at the feet of Jesus because we have failed to do His will and have made mistakes, but we are not to be discouraged. Even if we are overcome by the enemy, we are not cast off nor forsaken by God.

(18) WHAT IF WE FALL INTO SIN AFTER BEING BORN AGAIN?

____

____

1 John 2:1

____

____

____

____

____

1 John 1:9

Christ is at the right hand of God, He is there to help us. Do not forget the words of Jesus, "The Father Himself loveth you." John 16:27. He wants to bring us back to Himself. He wants to see His holiness revealed in us. And if we will just give ourselves to Him, He that has started to do good things in us will keep doing them until the day of Jesus Christ. We must pray with more effort and believe more fully. Then, as we begin to distrust our own power, we will more fully trust the power of our Redeemer and we will praise Him who reveals His goodness in us.

(19) AFTER WE ARE BORN AGAIN WHAT WILL WE REALIZE?

____

____

____

Isaiah 64:6

The closer you come to Jesus, the more sinful you will seem in your own eyes. Your faults will clearly be seen in contrast to His perfect nature. This shows proof that Satan's tricks have lost their power and that the life-giving power of the Spirit of God is awakening in you.

No deep-rooted love for Jesus can live in the heart of someone that does not see his own sinfulness. The person that is changed by the grace of Jesus will admire His holy character. If we do not see the bad in ourselves, this clearly shows that we have not seen the beauty and goodness of Jesus.

The less we see of that which we think is good in ourselves, the more we will see to admire in the endless purity and loveliness of Jesus our Saviour. The realization of our own sinfulness will bring us to Him who can forgive. When we realize our need for help and reach out to Jesus, He will show how powerful He is. The more our sense of need drives us to Jesus and to the Word of God, the clearer we will see how good He is and the more closely we will reflect His image.

The more time I spend contemplating the pure character of Christ the more I see my sinfulness. I long for a righteous and pure heart that only the creative power of Christ can restore in me.

Circle: Yes No Undecided

I choose, by His grace, to walk in Christ's footsteps and follow Him as my master. My prayer is that the fruits of His Spirit will be seen in me so that I may reflect His righteous and holy character.

Circle: Yes No Undecided

Study notes: ______________________________

Spiritual Growth

Lesson 8

(1) AS NEW BABES IN CHRIST, HOW IS OUR RELATIONSHIP WITH HIM DEVELOPED?

____

____

____

1 Peter 2:2

When we have a change of heart we become children of God and the Bible calls this being born again. You can compare it to the growing of the good seed in the parable of Jesus that was planted by the farmer. In the same way those who have just given their hearts to Jesus are, "as newborn babes," to "grow up" to the stature of men and women in Christ Jesus. Or like the good seed planted in the field, they are to grow up and bring forth fruit. Isaiah says that they shall "be called trees of righteousness, the planting of the Lord, that He might be glorified." Isaiah 61:3. We are shown real life examples like these to help us to better understand the mysterious truths of spiritual life.

Even with all the wisdom and skill that man has he cannot make life in even the smallest object in nature. It is only by the life which God alone gives, that either a plant or animal can live. It is the same way with our spiritual lives: only through God is spiritual life awakened in our hearts. Unless we are "born again" we cannot have the life which Jesus came to give. John 3:3.

(2) WHY CAN'T WE CAUSE OUR OWN SPIRITUAL GROWTH?

____

____

____

1 Corinthians 2:14

Just as God is the Source of all life, it is the same with our spiritual life and growth. It is God who brings the buds to bloom and gives fruit. It is by His power that the seed develops, "first the blade, then the ear, after that the full corn in the ear." Mark 4:28. And the prophet Hosea says of Israel, that "he shall grow as the lily." "They shall revive as the corn, and grow as the vine." Hosea 14:5, 7. Jesus tells us "consider the lilies how they grow." Luke 12:27. The plants and flowers do not grow by their own worry or effort, but by God's life-giving care. A child cannot make himself grow by worry or by his own power. It is the same way with our spiritual growth. We cannot grow spiritually by worry or by our own efforts.

(3) WHO IS THE ONLY SOURCE OF SPIRITUAL NOURISHMENT?

____

____

____

Psalms 84:11

____

____

____

Hosea 14:5

Both the plant and the child grow by getting from their surroundings the things they need for life. These things are air, sunshine, and food. What these gifts of nature are to the animal and plant, spiritually Jesus is to those who put their trust in Him. God has covered the whole world with the presence of His grace that is as real as the air which surrounds the earth. He did this by giving the unmatchable gift of His Son. Everyone who chooses to breathe this life-giving atmosphere will live and grow to be mature men and women in Christ Jesus.

When a flower grows it turns to the sun so that the bright beams may help make its beauty and symmetry complete. In the same way we should turn to the Sun of Righteousness so that heaven's light may shine upon us, and we may become more and more like Christ.

(4) HOW CAN WE CONTINUE TO GROW IN JESUS AND BE THE BEARER OF GOOD FRUIT?

____

____

John 15:5

Jesus teaches that we have to depend upon Him in order to live a holy life, just as the branch must depend upon the main vine to be able to grow and give fruit. When we are apart from Him we have no life; we have no power to resist when we are tempted; we cannot grow in grace and holiness. But when we walk with Him we can prosper. When we draw our life from Him, we will not wither or be without fruit. We will be like "a tree planted by the rivers of water." Psalms 1:3.

(5) HOW IS FAITH STRENGTHENED?

____

____

____

Hebrews 12:2

Many people think that they have to do the work alone. They have trusted in Jesus to be forgiven of their sins, but now they try by their own efforts to live the right way. Our own efforts will fail. Jesus says, "Without Me ye can do nothing." The way we grow in grace, our joy, and our usefulness all depend upon our bond with Jesus. It is by spending time with Him and abiding in Him each day and each hour that we can grow in grace. He is not only the Author, He is also the Finisher of our faith. We should make Jesus first, last, and always in all that we do. He is to be with us, not only at the beginning and the end of our journey, but at every step along the way.

(6) HOW DO WE CONTINUE TO ABIDE IN CHRIST?

____

____

____

Colossians 2:6

In the same way as we accepted Him at first, we continue to walk in Him. We gave ourselves to God to be totally His, to serve and obey Him, and we accepted Jesus as our Saviour. We could not make right our sins or change our own hearts. But since we gave ourselves to God, we believe that He, for Christ's sake, did all this for us. By faith we became Christ's and by faith we are to grow in Him. This growth will come by giving and taking as we walk with Him. We are to give our heart, our will, our service, and our obedience to Him. We must accept the fullness of all blessings which is Christ living in our hearts, to be our strength, our goodness, our everlasting helper, and to give us power to obey.

(7) WHY IS EARLY MORNING DEVOTIONAL SO IMPORTANT?

____

____

____

Proverbs 8:17

Give all of yourself to God each morning. Make this the very first thing you do. Let your prayer be, "Take all of me, O Lord, to be yours, I lay all my plans at Your feet, use me today in Your service. Walk with me and let all I do come from You." This is something that must be done each day. Each morning dedicate yourself to God for that day. Surrender all your plans to Him, let Him decide if they should be carried out or given up. By doing this day by day you will be giving your life into the hands of God, and will become more and more like Him.

(8) WHAT IS THE WAY TO KEEP PEACE IN OUR HEARTS?

____

____

____

Isaiah 26:3

____

____

____

____

____

2 Corinthians 3:18

A life in Christ is a life of peace. There may not always be excited feelings but there will always be a peaceful trust that stays with us. Our hope is not in ourselves, it is in Jesus. Our weakness is joined to His lasting strength, our lack of wisdom to His endless wisdom. We are not to look to ourselves. We should not think about self, but instead always look to Jesus. We should let our minds dwell on His love and on the beauty and perfection of His character. Think about how unselfish and humble He is. Think of how pure and holy He is. Think of His matchless love for all. It is by loving Him, copying Him, depending totally upon Him, that we are to be changed and become like Him.

(9) WHAT BLESSING HAS CHRIST PROMISED IF WE WILL COME TO HIM?

____

____

____

Matthew 11:28

Jesus says, "Abide in Me." These words bring to our mind the idea of rest, trust, and assurance in Him. And Isaiah gives the promise, "In quietness and in confidence shall be your strength." Isaiah 30:15. This rest is not found in doing nothing, for in the Saviour's invitation we are asked to "Take My yoke upon you: ...and ye shall find rest." Matthew 11:29. The heart that rests the most fully upon Jesus will be the one eager to do the most work for Him.

(10) WHAT SHOULD WE GUARD AGAINST IN OUR DAILY LIVES?

____

____

____

Psalms 37:7

When our mind is always thinking about the faults of others and dwelling on ourselves, it is turned away from Jesus who gives us life and strength. By this diversion Satan is always trying to keep us from thinking about our Saviour and staying close to Him. Satan tries to keep us thinking about the pleasures of this world, life's cares, difficulties and sorrows, the faults of others, or our own faults. All of these are the tools he uses to try to keep our minds from dwelling on Christ and being under his control.

(11) HOW CAN WE HAVE THE ASSURANCE OF KNOWING THAT WE HAVE ETERNAL LIFE?

____

____

____

____

1 John 5:12,13

Some people have a sensitive conscience and desire to live for God, but allow Satan to lead them to think about their own sins and weaknesses. By separating them from Jesus he hopes to win the victory. We should not be worrying about whether or not we will be saved. Doing that only turns our hearts away from Jesus who is our Source of strength. Give the keeping of your soul to God, and trust in Him. Always talk and think about Jesus. Let thoughts of yourself be lost in Him. Don't have any doubts and don't be afraid. Say with the apostle Paul, "I live; yet not I, but Christ liveth in me: and the life which I now live in the flesh I live by the faith of the Son of God, who loved me, and gave Himself for me." Galatians 2:20. Rest in God. He is able to keep you safe when you have given yourself to Him. If you will leave yourself in His hands, you will have the victory through Him that loves you.

(12) WHAT WILL HAPPEN TO THE RIGHTEOUS WHO CHOOSE TO RETURN TO SINFUL WAYS?

____

____

____

____

Ezekiel 18:24

When Jesus took on human nature, He bound us to Himself by a tie of love that can never be broken by any power. But we have the choice at any time not to accept it. Hebrews 10:29,39; Proverbs 28:18. Satan will always be trying to tempt us with things to cause this special tie to Jesus to be broken. He will be trying to get us to choose to separate ourselves from Jesus. This is where we need to watch and pray so that nothing can draw us to another master. 2 Peter 2:21,22. Because He loves us so much we are always free to choose, but let us keep our eyes fixed upon Jesus, and He will protect us. Looking unto Jesus we are safe.

(13) CAN ANYONE TAKE US OUT OF GOD'S HAND?

____

____

____

____

John 10:28

Nothing can pull us out of His hands of safety. When we are always looking unto Him, we "are changed into the same image from glory to glory, even as by the Spirit of the Lord." 2 Corinthians 3:18. It was by doing this that the early disciples became like our dear Saviour.

(14) WHEN WE HEAR THE CALL OF CHRIST HOW WILL WE FIND HIM?

____

____

____

Jeremiah 29:13

When the disciples heard the words of Jesus, they felt their need of Him. They searched, they found, and they followed Him. They went with Him everywhere: in the house, to the table, in private places, as well as public ones. They were with Him as students are with a teacher. Every day they received from His lips lessons of holy truth. They looked to Him, as servants do to their master, to learn their duty. It is their example we can follow.

(15) WERE THE DISCIPLES OF CHRIST GOOD BY NATURE, OR DID THEY GO THROUGH THE SAME STRUGGLES WE DO DURING CHRISTIAN GROWTH?

____

____

____

____

James 5:17

The disciples had the same battle to fight with sin. Romans 7:18,19. They needed the same grace in order to live a holy life. Even John, the "beloved" disciple, the one who came to reflect most closely the likeness of the Saviour, did not naturally have that beauty of character. He not only tried to put himself before others, he tried very hard to get glory for himself. He was also blind to good, and bitter when he was hurt. But as the character of Jesus was shown to him, he saw his own failures and became humble when he realized it. His heart was filled with admiration and love as he saw the strength, patience, power, tenderness, and meekness in the daily life of the Son of God. Day by day his heart was drawn closer to Jesus. He lost sight of self because of love for his Master. He gave his bitter and strong temper to Christ for Him to change. The rebuilding power of the Holy Spirit made his heart new. The power of the love of Jesus brought a change in his character. This is the sure result when we are one with Jesus. When Christ lives in our heart, our whole nature is changed. Christ's Spirit and His love softens our heart, tames our soul, and brings our thoughts and desires toward God and heaven.

(16) WHAT GREAT PROMISES OF COMFORT DID JESUS LEAVE FOR HIS FOLLOWERS?

____

____

____

____

Matthew 28:20

____

____

____

____

John 14:26

When Christ went to heaven, His followers could still feel His presence with them. It was a presence as if He were still there in person, full of love and light. Jesus the Saviour, who had walked, talked and prayed with them, who had spoken words of hope and comfort to their hearts, had been taken from them into heaven while this message of peace was still upon His lips. The sound of His voice had come back to them. As the cloud of angels greeted Him, He spoke the words, "Lo, I am with you always." He rose up to heaven in the form of a man. They knew that He was now before the throne of

God, and He was their Friend and Saviour still. They knew that His sympathies were unchanged and that He was still one with them. He could relate with those still in this suffering world. He was showing to God the merits of His own precious blood, showing His bloodstained hands and feet in remembrance of the price He had paid for those He saved. They knew that He went to heaven to prepare places for them, and He would come back again and take them to be with Him there.

(17) HOW IS JESUS ABLE TO ALWAYS BE IN THE HEARTS OF HIS CHILDREN?

___

___

___

___

___

___

___

John 14:16

As the followers of Jesus met together after He had risen to heaven, they were eager to bring their prayers to the Father in the name of Jesus. In deep respect and awe they bowed in prayer, claiming the promise of John 16:23, 24. They used their faith more and more and believed that "It is Christ that died, yea rather, that is risen again, who is even at the right hand of God, who also maketh intercession for us." Romans 8:34. Pentecost brought them the presence of the Comforter, of whom Jesus had said, He "shall be in you." He had also said, "It is expedient for you that I go away: for if I go not away, the Comforter will not come unto you; but if I depart, I will send Him unto you." John 14:17; 16:7. From that time forward through the Holy Spirit, Jesus would always be in the hearts of His children. They were closer now to Him than when He was there in person. The light, love, and power of Jesus living in them now was seen by others in such a way that, when they were with them they, "marveled; and they took knowledge of them, that they had been with Jesus." Acts 4:13.

(18) WERE CHRIST'S WORDS OF HOPE ONLY FOR THE DISCIPLES?

___

___

___

___

___

___

John 17:20

All that Jesus was to the disciples, He desires to be to His children today. In that last prayer, with the little group of disciples gathered around Him, He remembered us along with them. Jesus prayed for us, and He asked that we might be one with Him, just as He is one with the Father. What a union this is! Jesus said this about Himself, "The Son can do nothing of Himself" "the Father that dwelleth in Me, He doeth the works." John 5:19; 14:10.

(19) IF WE LIVE BY FAITH, SHARE WITH OTHERS, AND CONTINUE TO ABIDE WITH HIM WHAT WILL BE THE RESULT?

___

___

___

___

Ephesians 4:15

With Christ living in our hearts, He will work in us "both to will and to do of His good pleasure." Philippians 2:13. We will work as He worked and will show the same spirit. By loving Him and walking with Him, we will "grow up into Him in all things, which is the head, even Christ."

The Bible explains that at the point of my rebirth in Jesus I won't be a perfect and fully developed Christian. When I come to Him, I begin a growth process that takes a lifetime.

Circle: Yes No Undecided

I realize that in my relationship with Christ there is nothing I can do, neither worry or works, that will bring about my own spiritual growth.

Circle: Yes No Undecided

My part is to seek Him with my whole heart and put myself in His life-giving atmosphere. As I center my life around His leading as I abide in Him by faith, He will help me to grow in Him.

Circle: Yes No Undecided

I am grateful for the faithful guidance of the Spirit. It is my desire to always hear and follow Him so that I may live a life that will glorify the Father.

Circle: Yes No Undecided

The Bible teaches that when my thoughts, affections and desires are focused on Jesus I can have full confidence I have "the Son" and I have the assurance of eternal life.

Circle: Yes No Undecided

Study notes: ____

As a Friend

Because of the love God has given
me which has blessed my life so.

I feel now my special duty to tell you
what my Lord would have you know.

He's the one who gave my life its meaning,
He wants to do the same for you.

But before this can happen,
you must believe its true.

So as a friend I must be truthful,
because of the love He'd have me share.

I'll tell you how much better life can
be when we give Jesus our cares.

Sharing Our Faith

Lesson 9

(1) WHAT PRINCIPLE DOES JESUS INVITE US TO FOLLOW?

____

____

____

____

John 13:34

God is the one who gives life, light and joy to everything. He pours out blessings to all of His creatures like rays of light from the sun and streams of water bursting from a flowing spring. And whenever the love of God is in the heart, it will flow out to others in love and blessings.

Jesus' greatest joy is in lifting up and saving us from our sinful condition. Saving us was more important to Him than His own life, and He gave it for our sake. He suffered on the cross and took our shame. Angels are also always working for the happiness of others, for this is their joy. These sinless beings are always helping us, even though we are wretched and in every way lower in character and rank. The spirit of Christ's self-sacrificing love is the spirit that fills heaven with happiness. This is the spirit that Christ's followers will have.

When the love of Jesus is living in our heart, like a sweet smell it cannot be hidden. Its holy effect will be felt by those we are around. The spirit of Jesus in our heart is a spring in the desert which flows to refresh everyone, making those who are ready to die anxious to drink of the water of life.

(2) WHY DID JESUS COME TO EARTH?

____

____

____

Matthew 20:28

Our love to Jesus will be shown in a desire to work as He worked which was blessing and helping others. Following His example helps us to show love, tenderness, and sympathy toward all the creatures of our heavenly Father's care.

Jesus' life on earth was not a life of ease and selfishness. He worked with unending, earnest, and untiring effort to save those lost in sin. From the manger to Calvary He was always unselfish and did not try to avoid hard work. The pain he went through as He traveled and the untiring care He gave was always for the good of others. He said He "came not to be ministered unto, but to minister." This was the main reason for His life. Everything else came in second place. His purpose in life was to do the will of God and to finish His work. It was like food and water to Him. Selfishness had no part in the things He did.

(3) WHEN WE COME TO KNOW THE LOVE OF JESUS WHAT WILL BE THE DESIRE OF OUR HEARTS?

____

____

____

____

John 1:29

Those who accept the grace of Jesus will be ready to do anything they can so that others for whom Jesus died, may share in His heavenly gift. They will do all they can to make the world a better place because they were in it. To be this way is the result of a heart truly changed. As soon as we come to Christ there is born in our heart a desire to tell others what a precious friend we have found in Jesus. This saving and life changing truth cannot be shut up in our heart. If we are covered with the goodness of Jesus and are filled with the joy of His Spirit living in us, we will not be able to keep from telling others. If we have found or ourselves that the Lord is good we will have something to tell the world. We will do like Philip when he found the Saviour. We will invite others into His presence. We will show them attractive things about Jesus and describe to them the things we cannot yet see about a better world to come. We will have a strong desire to follow in the path that Jesus walked. We will have a real desire for those around us to "behold the Lamb of God" so that they, too, may come to know Him.

(4) WHAT IS THE RESULT OF UNSELFISH LABOR FOR OTHERS?

____

____

____

____

____

Proverbs 11:25

As we do things to help bless others it will result in blessings coming back upon ourselves. This was the reason God let us have a part to play in His plan to win back the lost. He has given us the honor of being able to partake of Christ's holy nature and then to share blessings with others. This is the highest honor and the greatest joy that it is possible for God to give to us. Those who in this way get involved in doing these acts of love are the ones who are brought nearest to their Creator.

God could have given the angels the joy of proclaiming the gospel or used other methods. But, in His endless love, He chose to let us become partners with Him in this loving ministry. He wanted us to share in the joy and spiritual blessings that comes from unselfishly serving others.

(5) WHAT UNSELFISH EXAMPLE DID CHRIST GIVE US?

___

___

___

2 Corinthians 8:9

We are brought into sympathy with Christ when we go through the kind of suffering He went through. Every time we deny ourselves and do a good deed for someone else this makes the desire of giving even stronger in our heart. When we do this we become closer to Jesus, the one who saved the world. He "was rich, yet for your sakes ... became poor, that ye through His poverty might be rich." And it is only when we minister to the needs of others that life can be a blessing to us. This was God's reason for creating us.

If you will go to work for Jesus in the way He wants His followers to, and win souls for Him, you will feel the need to be closer to Him. You will want to learn more about spiritual things and will have a hunger and thirst for good. You will plead with God, and your faith will be made stronger. Your soul will drink larger amounts of water from the well of life. When you come face to face with trials and things go wrong, this will drive you to spend more time in the Bible and in prayer. You will grow in grace, learn more about Jesus and draw closer to Him.

(6) WHO GIVES US THE DESIRE TO REACH OUT TO OTHERS?

___

___

___

___

Philippians 2:13

(7) WHAT BLESSINGS COME TO THOSE WHO HELP OTHERS?

___

___

___

___

___

Isaiah 58:10,11

The spirit of unselfishness shown by helping others develops, strengthens, and gives Christ-like loveliness to the character. It brings peace and happiness to the one who has it. As a result our goals are set higher and there is no room for laziness or selfishness. When we exercise these Christ-like ways we will grow and become stronger in our work for God. We will have a clearer understanding of spiritual things, our faith will be steady and grow, and we will receive more power in our prayers. The Spirit of God, moving in our spirit, brings together holy things in our hearts as we are touched in a divine way. When we apply ourselves in this way to do unselfish things for the good of others we are most certainly choosing the way of salvation.

(8) WHAT SHOULD WE DO TO STRENGTHEN OUR GROWTH IN CHRIST?

___

___

___

___

James 1:25

The only way to grow in grace is to be doing the work which Jesus has asked us to do. Without being partial to anyone, we should help others the best we can. We can do this by blessing those who are in need with whatever help we can give them. Strength comes by exercise and activity which gives us spiritual life. Some people try to carry on a Christian life by just sitting by and accepting the blessings that come from the grace of Jesus. When they are doing nothing for Jesus they are simply trying to live by eating without working. It is the same in the spiritual world as it is in the regular world; this passiveness always results in loss and decay. If you refuse to exercise your arms and legs you will soon lose the power to use them. It is the same way with Christians who do not exercise their God-given powers. They not only fail to grow to know Christ, but they lose the strength that they already had.

(9) WHAT INSTRUCTIONS HAS CHRIST GIVEN THE CHURCH?

____

____

____

____

____

Matthew 28:19

The church of Jesus is God's chosen tool that he uses to save men. The job of the church is to carry the gospel to the world. By using the talents we are given, we are to spread the gospel as Jesus has asked us to do. Once we have had the love of Jesus shown to us, we owe it to those who don't know Him to tell them about His love. God has given us light, not just for ourselves but to spread to others.

If all the followers of Christ were doing their duty, there would be thousands where there is only one telling the gospel in heathen lands today. And if all who could not personally help with the work would support it with their money, their sympathy, and their prayers, there would be far more earnest work and results in saving souls.

(10) DO WE HAVE TO GO TO A FAR AWAY MISSION FIELD TO SHARE JESUS WITH OTHERS?

____

____

____

____

1 Corinthians 7:24

We don't need to go to heathen lands, or even leave the narrow circle of the home, if this is where our duty is to work for Christ. We can work for Him in our homes, in the church, with those that we are around, and with those that we do business with.

The greater part of our Saviour's life on earth was spent in patient work in the carpenter's shop at Nazareth. Helpful angels were with the Lord of Life as He walked side by side with common people and workers. No one knew who He was or gave Him honor. Whether He was working at His humble job, healing the sick, or walking upon the storm-tossed waves of Galilee, He always faithfully did the task He was sent from heaven to do. We can follow His example and in the humblest duties and lowest positions of life, we may walk and work with Jesus.

The apostle Paul says, "Let every man, wherein he is called, therein abide with God." If we are businessmen we may do our business in a way that will glorify our Master by our faithfulness. If we are true followers of Jesus we will carry our faith into everything we do and show others what Jesus is like. The mechanic may be a hard working and faithful example of Jesus who worked in a typical livelihood among the hills of Galilee. Everyone who claims to be Christian should work so that others, by seeing his good works, may be led to bring glory to their Creator and Redeemer.

(11) WHAT WILL HAPPEN TO THE TALENTS THAT WE ARE GIVEN AND DON'T USE?

____

____

____

Matthew 25:28,29

Many people make excuses for not using their gifts for the service of Jesus because others have greater ability and other advantages that they don't have. Many people think that only those who are very talented need to dedicate their abilities to the service of God. It has come to be understood by many that talents are given to only a certain chosen group and the rest are not included to share in the work or the rewards. But it is not this way in the story Jesus told. When the master of the house called on his servants, he gave to every one their work to do.

(12) HOW CAN OUR LOVE FOR CHRIST BE A BLESSING TO OTHERS?

____

____

____

____

Ephesians 6:6,7

With a loving spirit we may do life's humblest duties for God. If the love of God is in the heart, it will be shown in the life. The sweet presence of Jesus will be all around us and the influence we have will lift up others and bless them.

(13) IF OUR RELATIONSHIP IS RIGHT WITH GOD WHAT WILL OUR DESIRE BE ?

____

____

____

Colossians 3:23

We are not to wait for great events or expect to have great abilities before we can go to work for God. We don't need to worry about what the world will think. When our daily life shows how pure and sincere our faith is, then others will be convinced that our desire is to help them and our efforts will not be lost.

(14) WHAT WILL RESULT FROM A LIFE OF FAITH AND SHARING?

____

____

____

2 Corinthians 9:6

The humblest and poorest of the followers of Jesus can be a blessing to others even though they may not realize they are doing any special good. They may not know that by their influence they may start waves of blessings that will grow wider and deeper. The blessed results they may never know until the day that the final rewards are given. They do not feel or know that they are doing anything great. They are not supposed to weary themselves with worry about whether their efforts will be a success. They only have to go forward quietly, doing faithfully the work that God's plan for them gives. If they do this their lives will not be in vain. Their own souls will be growing more and more into the likeness of Christ. They are workers together with God in this life, and by doing this are being prepared for the higher work and the unshadowed joy of the life to come.

I am thankful to Jesus for leaving the glory of heaven to minister to the needs of mankind.

Circle: Yes No Undecided

I am realizing the Bible teaches that the richest spiritual blessings and growth will come to those who minister to others.

Circle: Yes No Undecided

I pray for the Holy Spirit to guide me to follow Christ's example of evangelism: first, to mingle with people and be a friend; second, to show compassion for their physical needs and gain their confidence; and then tell them the good news of the gospel.

Circle: Yes No Undecided

I dedicate my life to God's service and pray that He will guide me into ministry for others.

Circle: Yes No Undecided

In Your Presence

You, Lord, caress the sea with
your fingertips and supply faith-
fully to all the flock their feed.

You hold your people in your palm
protectively, and do everything
to meet their smallest need.

By the wind we feel Your breath upon
our faces. By the reflections of the
waters You are seen.

By the whistle of a robin we do
hear You, and where the mountains
reach the sky there is Your touch.

What can be said to glorify
Your greatness? What can be
done to lift up high Your love?

There is nothing men can do
themselves alone to display
Your presence like the
way You've already shown.

Learning More About God

(1) WHAT IS AN EVER PRESENT SOURCE THAT REVEALS GOD'S LOVE?

____

____

____

____

Psalms 19:1

There are many ways in which God is seeking to make Himself known to us and bring us closer to Him. Nature is always speaking to our senses. The open heart will be moved with the love and glory of God as we see it shown to us through the works of His hands. The listening ear can hear and understand God speaking through nature. The green fields, the tall trees, the buds and flowers, the passing clouds, the falling rain, and the babbling brook declare the Creator's love. These glories of the heavens speak to our hearts and invite us to get to know Him who made them all.

Our Saviour tied together His precious lessons of love with the things of nature. The trees, the birds, the flowers of the valleys, the hills, the lakes, and the beautiful heavens, as well as the things that happen and the things around us in our daily life were all joined with the words of truth. These lessons can often be recalled to our mind, even in the middle of the busy cares of our life of labor.

God wants His children to see the value in the things He has done, and delight in the simple and quiet beauty with which He has decorated our earthly home. God loves beautiful things, but even more than outward beauty He loves beauty of character. It is His desire that we become pure and simple like the quiet beauty of the flowers.

(2) IN THE MIDST OF OUR BUSY LIVES HOW CAN WE HEAR GOD SPEAKING TO US IN NATURE?

____

____

Psalms 4:4,5

If we will just listen, the things God has created will teach us very important lessons of how to obey and trust. We can see that the things of nature obey the will of God from the stars that, throughout time, travel in their appointed path, clear down to the smallest atom.

(3) HOW DOES GOD SHOW THAT EVERY CREATURE IS SPECIAL TO HIM?

____

____

____

Matthew 10:30

God is the Creator who cares for everything. He who holds up the unnumbered worlds in space, and at the same time cares for the needs of the little brown sparrow that sings it's humble song. When we go out to do our daily work, when we pray, when we lie down at night, when we get up in the morning, when the rich man feasts in his mansion, or when the poor man gathers his children around a humble table, each is tenderly watched over by our heavenly Father. There is no tear shed that He does not see and no smile that goes unnoticed.

(4) WHEN WE COME TO KNOW THE LORD AND TRUST OUR LIVES IN HIS HANDS WHAT SECURITY DO WE HAVE?

____

____

____

____

____

Romans 8:28

If we would just fully believe this, we would let go of all undue worry. If everything, whether great or small, were left in the hands of God, our lives would not be filled with so much disappointment. He is not puzzled by our many problems and He is not overwhelmed by their weight. When we realize this we can enjoy a peace in our heart which many do not know.

(5) HOW DOES NATURE REVEAL GOD'S LOVE?

____

____

____

1 Corinthians 2:9

When your senses are enjoying the pleasing and lovely things of this earth, think of the world that will come. The new world will never know the results of sin and death, and the face of nature will not wear the shadow of its curse. In your thoughts picture the home of the ones who are saved and remember that it will be more glorious than your dreams. In the different gifts that God has given us in nature we can only see the faintest gleaming of His glory.

The poet and the naturalist have many things to say about nature, but it is the Christian who enjoys the beauty of the earth with the highest appreciation. He notices his Father's handiwork and sees His love in the flowers, shrubs and trees. No one can fully appreciate the meaning of a hill or a valley, a river or the sea, unless he sees them as a way God is showing His love to man.

(6) AS WE GET TO KNOW GOD WHAT LESSONS WILL BECOME EVIDENT?

____

____

____

____

____

____

Psalms 33:5

God speaks to us through the way He works in our lives and through the working of His Spirit upon our hearts. In our affairs and surroundings, in the changes that take place every day around us, we may find precious lessons if our hearts are just open to see them.

(7) WHY ARE THE EXPERIENCES OF THE PATRIARCHS AND PROPHETS RECORDED IN SCRIPTURE?

____

____

____

____

____

Romans 15:4

God speaks to us in His word. In it we are clearly told what His character is like. We are shown how He deals with men, and about His great plan to redeem us. In it we are shown the history of the patriarchs and prophets and other holy men of long ago. They were men "subject to like passions as we are." James 5:17. We see how they struggled through tough times like our own, and how they fell under temptation as we have done. We also can see how they took heart again and won the victories through the grace of God. By seeing, we are encouraged in our search after righteousness. We read of the valuable experiences they were given, of the light and love and blessing that they were able to enjoy and of the work they were able to do through the grace they were given. When we see these things the spirit that inspired them kindles a flame of holy envy in our hearts. We will desire to be like them in character and to walk with God as they did.

(8) WHAT SPECIAL BLESSINGS ARE REVEALED BY STUDY OF THE SCRIPTURES?

____

____

____

John 5:39

Jesus said of the Old Testament Scriptures, "They are they which testify of Me," and it is even more so of the New. Yes, the whole Bible tells of Christ the Redeemer; He in whom our hopes of eternal life are centered. From the first record of creation, for "without Him was not anything made that was made," to the closing promise, "Behold, I come quickly," we are reading of His works and listening to His voice. John 1:3; Revelation 22:12. If you want to get to know the Saviour, study the Holy Scriptures.

(9) WHY IS GETTING TO KNOW GOD THROUGH HIS WORD VERY IMPORTANT?

____

____

____

____

John 6:63

Fill your whole heart with the words of God. This is the living Water that can satisfy your burning thirst. This is the living Bread from heaven. Jesus says, "Except ye eat the flesh of the Son of man, and drink His blood, ye have no life in you." John 6:53. Our bodies are made from what we eat and drink, so what we put into them affects our physical health. It is the same way with our spiritual health. It is what we dwell upon that will give tone and strength to our spiritual life.

(10) WHAT MAGNIFICENT THEME OF THE BIBLE SHOULD WE DWELL ON?

____

____

1 Corinthians 2:2

The story of salvation is one that the angels desire to look into. It will be the study and the song of those who have been saved throughout the endless ages of eternity. Isn't it important enough for our careful thought and study now? The endless mercy and love of Jesus, the sacrifice made for us; these themes deserve the most serious and earnest thought. We should think about the character of our dear Redeemer and Advocate. We should think about the purpose of the One who came to save His people from their sins. As we think about these heavenly truths, our faith and love will grow stronger. Our prayers will be more and more favorable to God; they will become more and more mixed with faith and love; they will be intelligent and earnest. There will be more constant trust in Jesus, and a real daily experience in His power to "save to the uttermost" all who come unto God by Him.

(11) WHAT TYPE OF INFLUENCES STRENGTHENS OUR CHARACTER?

____

____

____

____

____

Philippians 4:8

(12) AS WE MEDITATE ON GOD'S HOLINESS WHAT DESIRE WILL FILL OUR HEART?

____

____

____

1 Corinthians 15:49

As we think about how perfect Jesus is, we will want to be totally changed and made new in His pure image. 2 Corinthians 3:18. There will be a hunger and thirst in us to become like Jesus, the One whom we adore. The more our thoughts are focused on Jesus, the greater our desire will be to tell others about Him and to reflect His character.

(13) FOR WHOM WAS THE WORD OF GOD WRITTEN?

____

____

Psalms 19:7

The Bible was not written only for the scholar, in fact, it is just the opposite; it was written for the common people. The great truths are made as clear as day. No one will make the mistake and lose their way except those who follow their own judgment instead of the plain will of God which is evident in His Word.

(14) WHY IS PERSONAL STUDY OF GOD'S WORD SO ESSENTIAL?

____

____

____

____

2 Timothy 2:15

We should not just listen to what other men say the Bible teaches, but we should study the words of God for ourselves. If we allow others to do our thinking, we will have weak desires and limited abilities. The high powers of our mind may be so stunted by lack of exercise on thoughts that are worthy, that we lose our ability to grasp the deeper meaning of the Word of God. The mind will be made stronger if it is used to study out the subjects of the Bible, comparing scripture with scripture and spiritual things with spiritual things.

There is nothing that works better to strengthen the mind than the study of the Scriptures. No other book is so powerful to raise the thoughts, and to give energy to our abilities as the broad, uplifting truths of the Bible. If we would study God's Word as we should, we would have a fullness of mind, a greatness of character, and a very stable purpose which is rarely seen in these times.

(15) WHAT TYPE OF STUDY WILL BENEFIT US THE MOST?

____

____

Psalms 119:11

If we read the Scriptures in a hurry there isn't much good that will come from reading them. One may read the whole Bible through and still fail to see its beauty or understand its deep and hidden meaning. One verse studied until its importance is clear to our mind and until we understand how it relates to the plan to save us, is worth more than reading many chapters with no exact purpose in mind and no positive wisdom gained. Keep your Bible with you and any time you have the chance read and memorize Scripture. Even while you are walking down the street you may read a verse and think about it and in this way fix it in your mind.

(16) HOW SHOULD STUDY OF THE BIBLE BE APPROACHED?

____

____

Isaiah 28:10

We cannot gain wisdom without strong efforts and prayerful study. Some parts of Scripture are very plain and can't be misunderstood, but there are others where the meaning does not lie on the surface to be seen at a glance. Scripture must be compared with scripture. We should study each text carefully and prayerfully think about it. When this is done we will be richly blessed. Just like the miner who finds veins of precious metal hidden under the surface of the earth, the one who keeps on searching the Word of God, as if searching for hidden treasure, will find truths of the greatest value. They will find great truths that are not found by the careless seeker. These inspired words when meditated upon will be like streams flowing from the fountain of life.

(17) WHY IS PRAYER IMPORTANT BEFORE WE STUDY THE HOLY SCRIPTURES?

____

____

____

____

Jeremiah 33:3

The Bible should never be studied without prayer. Before opening its pages we should ask for the Holy Spirit to open our minds to be able to understand and it will be done. When Nathanael came to Jesus, the Saviour said, "Behold an Israelite indeed, in whom is no guile!" Nathanael said, "Whence knowest Thou me?" Jesus answered, "Before that Philip called thee, when thou wast under the fig tree, I saw thee." John 1:47, 48. Jesus will see us also in the secret places of prayer if we will ask for wisdom so that we may know what truth is. Angels from heaven will be with those who humbly seek the Lord for guidance.

(18) HOW IS TRUTH REVEALED?

____

____

____

John 16:13

The Holy Spirit lifts up and brings glory to the Saviour. It is His goal to show us Jesus, the purity of His goodness, and the great gift of life that we have through Him. Jesus says, "He shall receive of Mine, and shall show it unto you." The Holy Spirit who is the Spirit of Truth is the only effective Teacher of heavenly truth. God must really love us to give His Son to die for us and to send His Spirit to be our Teacher and our continual Guide.

I am amazed God loves me so much that if I were the only sinner, He would have sent His Son to die just for me.

Circle: Yes No Undecided

I am grateful God has provided His Word to help me know Him better. It is my source of wisdom, and it reveals the way that I may have eternal life.

Circle: Yes No Undecided

In God's Word I find learning, patience, comfort, and hope. I ask Him for a burning desire to study it so that I may hide His truth in my heart and not sin against Him.

Circle: Yes No Undecided

I pray for the Holy Spirit to be my teacher and to give me a humble heart. I pray for wisdom so that I may correctly put line upon line and precept upon precept and understand truth.

Circle: Yes No Undecided

It is my goal to seek the Lord with all my heart, mind and soul. It is the desire of my heart to hear the leading of the Holy Spirit so that I may follow the light that the Scriptures shed on the path of eternal life.

Circle: Yes No Undecided

Study notes: ______________________________

The Privilege of Prayer

(1) WHY IS CONTACT WITH GOD THROUGH PRAYER SO IMPORTANT?

Jeremiah 29:12

Through nature, His working in our lives, and by the power of His Spirit God speaks to us. But all this is not enough. We also need to pour out our hearts to Him. In order to have spiritual life and energy, we must have personal contact with our heavenly Father. Our minds may be drawn toward Him and we may think about His works, His mercies, and His blessings, but this is not enough. In order for us to be fully in touch with God, we must share with Him the things that happen in our daily lives.

Prayer is opening up our hearts to God like we would to a friend. It is not needed as a way for us to make things known to Him; He already knows all things. The purpose is to allow us to receive Him. The act of prayer does not bring God down to us, it is the means by which we are brought up to Him.

(2) WHAT HAS JESUS INVITED US TO DO AS WE COME TO HIM IN PRAYER?

1 Peter 5:7

When Jesus was here on earth He taught His followers how to pray. He told them to tell God what their daily needs were, and to "cast all their care upon Him." The promise He gave them that their petitions will be heard is also for us.

(3) HOW OFTEN SHOULD OUR HEARTS HAVE COMMUNICATION WITH GOD IN PRAYER?

___

___

___

Luke 18:1

While Jesus lived among men He prayed often. Jesus our Saviour saw first hand what our needs and weakness are. He became a prayer warrior asking His Father for fresh supplies of strength so that He could be ready for His duties and trials. He is our example in all things. He was "in all points tempted like as we are." But as the One without sin, His nature pulled back from evil and He made it through the struggles and torture of His soul in this world full of sin. His humanity made prayer a necessity and a privilege. He found comfort and joy in communicating with His Father. If the Saviour of men who was the Son of God felt the need of prayer, just think how much more we, as weak and sinful mortals, should feel the need to always be praying earnestly.

(4) HOW SHOULD WE COME TO GOD IN PRAYER?

___

___

Hebrews 4:16

Our heavenly Father is waiting to pour out on us the fullness of His blessings. It is our privilege to drink as much as we want from His fountain of endless love. Isn't it amazing that we choose to pray so little? God is ready and willing to hear the sincere prayer of the humblest of His children, but we stubbornly refuse to make known our needs to Him or give Him the praise He deserves. It makes you wonder what the angels of heaven think of us poor helpless, human beings. We are exposed to temptation and yet we pray so very little and have so little faith, when God's heart of infinite love yearns toward us, ready to give us more than they can ask or even imagine. The angels love to bow before God and they love to be near Him; they consider closeness with God their greatest joy. Isn't it amazing that His children on earth, who need so much more of the help that only God can give, seem satisfied to walk without the light of His Spirit and the companionship of His presence?

(5) WHAT ARE THE TWO KEYS TO OVERCOMING TEMPTATION?

___

___

Matthew 26:41

The darkness of the evil one surrounds those who neglect to pray. They are drawn into sin by whispered temptations, and it is all because they do not use the privilege of prayer that God has given them. Why should we as sons and daughters of God be unwilling to pray when prayer is the key in the hand of faith to unlock heaven's storehouse where there is an unlimited amount of power? If we do not continuously pray and carefully watch we are in danger of growing careless, causing us to leave the right path. The enemy is always trying to block the way to the mercy seat. He doesn't want us, by earnest prayer and faith, to receive the grace and power to resist when we are tempted.

(6) WHAT MUST BE OUR SPIRITUAL CONDITION FOR GOD TO ANSWER OUR PRAYERS?

___

___

___

Isaiah 44:3

When we pray under certain conditions, we can know and expect that God will hear and answer our prayers. One of these conditions is that we must feel our need of His help. He has promised, "I will pour water upon him that is thirsty, and floods upon the dry ground." Those who hunger and thirst for what is right and who long after God can be sure that they will be filled. Our heart must be open to the Holy Spirit's power, or God's blessing cannot be received.

(7) WHAT IS THE SECOND CONDITION FOR RECEIVING ANSWERED PRAYERS?

____

____

____

Luke 11:9

Our great need is itself an argument and a plea. We should go to the Lord and ask Him for the things we need. "Ask, and it shall be given you." And "He that spared not His own Son, but delivered Him up for us all, how shall He not with Him also freely give us all things?" Matthew 7:7; Romans 8:32

(8) HOW DOES REBELLION AFFECT OUR PRAYERS?

____

____

____

____

____

Proverbs 28:9

If we hold evil in our hearts, if we hold on to any known sin, the Lord will not hear us. Proverbs 15:8. However, the prayer of someone who is really sorry for his sin is always accepted. When we have made right all the things we have done that we know are wrong, we can believe that God will answer our prayers. Our goodness will never bring us in favor with God. It is only the goodness of Jesus that will save us. It is only His blood that can make us clean, but we still have to do our part and meet the conditions of acceptance.

(9) WHAT IS THE NEXT STEP IN RECEIVING ANSWERS TO OUR PRAYERS?

____

____

____

James 1:6

____

____

____

Mark 11:24

Faith is another important condition to answered prayer. Do we take Him at His word? The promise is broad and has no limit, and He is faithful who made the promise. When we do not receive the exact things we asked for, right at the time we ask, we should still believe that the Lord hears and that He will answer our prayers. We are so much in error and are so short-sighted that we sometimes ask for things that would not be a blessing to us. In love, our heavenly Father answers our prayers by giving us what will be for our best interest. He gives us what we would desire if, through heaven's eyes, we could see all things as they really are. When it seems as if our prayers have not been answered, we are to hold on to the promise because the time of answering will surely come. We shall receive the blessing we needed most. To claim that our prayers will always be answered in the exact way and for the exact thing that we desire is presumption. God is too wise to be wrong, and too good to keep any good thing from them that walk uprightly. Do not fear to trust Him, even though you do not see the instant answer to your prayers. Trust upon His sure promise.

(10) WHAT GREAT PROMISE ARE WE GIVEN?

____

____

____

____

____

Matthew 7:7

If we keep dwelling on our doubts and fears, or try to explain everything that we cannot see clearly, doubt will only increase and grow deeper. It is better to come to God feeling helpless and dependent as we really are. In humble and trusting faith we can make known our needs to Him whose knowledge is unlimited. He is the One who sees everything in creation; who controls everything by His Will and Word and He will answer our cry and will let light shine into our hearts. Through sincere prayer we are brought into touch with the mind of the Infinite. We may have no obvious sign right at the time that the face of Jesus is bending over us in concern and love, but it is true. We may not feel His visible touch, but His hand is upon us in love and pitying tenderness.

(11) HOW IS OUR FORGIVENESS FROM GOD DETERMINED?

____

____

____

Matthew 6:12

When we come in prayer to ask mercy and blessings from God we should have a spirit of love and forgiveness in our own hearts. How can we pray, "Forgive us our debts, as we forgive our debtors," and keep within us an unforgiving spirit? If we expect our own prayers to be heard we must forgive others in the same way and to the same extent as we desire to be forgiven.

(12) HOW OFTEN SHOULD WE PRAY?

____

____

____

Colossians 4:2

Perseverance in prayer is also a condition of receiving our answer. We must always pray that we can grow in faith and experience. We are to be "instant in prayer." Romans 12:12. Peter tells believers to be "sober, and watch unto prayer." 1 Peter 4:7. Paul directs, "In everything by prayer and supplication with thanksgiving let your requests be made known unto God." Philippians 4:6. "But ye, beloved," says Jude, "praying in the Holy Ghost, keep yourselves in the love of God." Jude 20,21. Unceasing prayer is the unbroken union of our soul with God, so that life from God flows into our life, and from our life, purity and holiness flow back to God.

There is a need for us to be diligent in prayer and not let anything hinder us. We should make every effort to keep contact between Jesus and ourselves. Look for any opportunity to go where prayer can be made. Those who are really seeking for communion with God will be seen in prayer meetings, faithful to do their duty and earnest and anxious to reap all the good they can gain. They will take any and every opportunity to place themselves where they can receive rays of light from heaven.

(13) WHY IS PRIVATE PRAYER SO ESSENTIAL?

____

____

____

____

____

____

Matthew 6:6

We should pray in the family circle, but above all we must not neglect secret prayer, for this is what gives life to our soul. It is impossible for our soul to prosper if we do not pray. Family prayers or prayers in public are by themselves not enough. When you are alone let your soul be laid open to the inspecting eye of God. Secret prayer is to be heard only by our prayer-hearing God. No curious ears are to hear our requests. In secret prayer the soul is free from excitement and distracting influences around us. Calmly, but earnestly, our prayer will reach out to God. Sweet and sure will be the effect flowing back from Him who sees in secret, and whose ear is open to hear the prayer coming from our heart. By calm and simple faith our soul touches God and gathers rays of heavenly light which strengthens and keeps it going in the battle against Satan. God is our tower of strength.

Pray in private, and as you go about your daily work, often let your heart be uplifted to God. This is how Enoch walked with Him. These silent prayers rise like precious incense before God's throne of grace. Satan cannot overcome one whose heart is fixed upon God.

(14) IS THERE EVER A TIME WHEN PRAYER IS NOT APPROPRIATE?

____

____

____

1 Thessalonians 5:17

There is not a time or place where it is not proper to offer up a prayer to God. There is nothing that can keep us from lifting up our hearts in the spirit of earnest prayer. When we are in the crowds on the street or in the middle of a business meeting, we may send up a request to God and plead for heaven's guidance. That is what Nehemiah did when he made his request before King Artaxerxes. A special connection may be found wherever we are. We should have the door of our heart open all the time and our invitation going up that Jesus may come and stay as a heavenly guest in the soul.

Even when there is an ungodly and corrupt atmosphere around us, we don't have to breathe its poison. We can live in the pure air of heaven. We may close every door to impure and unholy thoughts by lifting our soul into the presence of God through sincere prayer. Those whose hearts are willing to receive the support and blessing of God will walk in a holier atmosphere than that of earth and will always be in touch with heaven.

(15) WHEN WE ARE IN CONSTANT COMMUNICATION WITH OUR LORD WHAT IS THE RESULT?

____

____

____

____

Philippians 4:6,7

We need to have a clearer view of Jesus and a fuller understanding of the value of eternal life. The beauty of holiness is to fill the hearts of God's children, but for this to take place, we should look for a divine revealing of heavenly things.

We should let our soul be drawn out and upward so that God may grant us a breath of the heavenly atmosphere. We can choose to keep so near to God that in every unexpected trial our thoughts will turn to Him in the same natural way that the flower turns to the sun.

(16) WHAT INVITATION DOES GOD SO GRACIOUSLY EXTEND TO EVERY LONGING SOUL?

____

____

____

Psalms 147:3

Take your wants, your joys, your sorrows, your cares, and your fears before God. You cannot weight Him down; you cannot make Him weary. He is the One who numbers the hairs of your head and He is not unresponsive to the needs of His children. "The Lord is very pitiful, and of tender mercy." James 5:11. His heart of love is touched by our sorrows and even more by telling Him of them. We should take to Him in prayer everything that puzzles the mind. Nothing is too great for Him to bear. He holds up worlds, and rules over all the affairs of the universe. Nothing that in any way concerns our peace is too small for Him to notice.

There is no part of our lives that is too dark for Him to see, nor is a problem too difficult for Him to solve. No hardship can come upon the least of His children, no anxiety that troubles the soul, no joy give us cheer, no sincere prayer from our lips, that does not touch His heart of love. The relationship between God and each one of us is as close and as secure as if there were not another soul upon the earth to share His watch-care, or another soul for whom He gave His beloved Son.

(17) IN WHOSE NAME SHOULD WE PRAY?

____

____

John 15:16

Jesus said, "Ye shall ask in My name: and I say not unto you, that I will pray the Father for you: for the Father Himself loveth you." John 16:26, 27. But to pray in the name of Jesus is much more than just a mere mention of His name at the beginning and the ending of a prayer. It is to pray in the mind and spirit of Jesus, while believing in His promises, trusting in His grace, and doing His works.

(18) WHAT SHOULD BE COMBINED WITH PRAYER AND WORSHIP?

____

____

____

James 1:27

____

____

____

Matthew 28:19

God does not want any of us to become hermits or monks and hide from the world in order to devote ourselves to acts of worship. The life must be like Christ's life, which was shared between the privacy of the mountains and the multitude of people. Someone who does nothing but pray will soon stop praying, or his prayers will become the same ones over and over. When people take themselves out of social life, away from the world of Christian duty and cross carrying, when they stop working earnestly for the Lord, who worked earnestly for them, they don't have anything to pray about and have no purpose for their devotion. Their prayers become personal and selfish. They cannot pray about the needs of humanity or the strengthening of the kingdom of Christ.

(19) WHAT IS THE PURPOSE OF CHRISTIAN FELLOWSHIP?

____

____

____

Hebrews 10:25

We are the ones who will lose when we neglect the privilege of coming together to strengthen and encourage one another in the service of God. The truths of His Word lose their clearness and importance in our minds. Our hearts are no longer learning nor awakened to the cleansing power of God's Word. Separating ourselves from other Christians will weaken our sympathy for others. If we stay to ourselves we are not doing the job that God planned for us to do. We will eventually lose our spirituality. The right development of the social part of our nature helps us to sympathize with others and this strengthens and develops us for the service of God.

When we as Christians spend time telling each other about the love of God and the precious truths of God's saving plan for us, our hearts are refreshed. When we have fellowship we are learning more about our heavenly Father and are receiving a renewed glimpse of His grace. Our desire grows to tell the world about His love, and as we do this our own hearts are warmed and encouraged. When we think and talk more about Jesus and less about ourselves, we have a lot more of His presence with us.

(20) WHO SHOULD THE CENTER OF OUR THOUGHTS AND AFFECTIONS BE ON?

____

____

____

Isaiah 26:3,4

If we would just think about God as often as we have signs of His care for us we would always have Him in our thoughts and we would enjoy talking about Him and giving Him praise. We talk of passing things of this world because we are interested in them. We talk about our friends because we love them. Our joys and our sorrows are connected with them, yet we have much greater reason to love God than to love our earthly friends. It should be the most natural thing in the world to put Him first in all our thoughts, to talk of His goodness and tell others of His power. The rich gifts He has given to us were not meant to absorb our thoughts and love so much that we would have nothing to give to God. They are to constantly remind us of Him and to bring us closer with ties of love and gratefulness to our heavenly Father who provides for us. Our thoughts tend to stay close to this earth. Let us look up to the open door of the sanctuary in heaven, where the light of the glory from God shines in the face of Jesus, who "is able also to save them to the uttermost that come unto God by Him." Hebrews 7:25.

(21) WHAT IS AN IMPORTANT ELEMENT OF PRAYER?

____

____

____

____

____

Philippians 4:6

We need to praise God more "for His goodness, and His wonderful works to the children of men." Psalms 107:8. Our daily devotional time should not primarily consist of asking and receiving. We should not always be thinking of what we want and never think about blessings we receive. We certainly do not pray too much and we do not show the appreciation we should to our Heavenly Father. We are always receiving God's mercies but give Him very little thanks in return! How little we praise Him for what He has done for us.

(22) WHAT WILL BE THE RESULT WHEN WE JOYFULLY DEDICATE OUR LIFE TO CHRIST?

____

____

____

____

____

Deuteronomy 12:7

In times past the Lord told Israel the importance of serving Him with a glad heart. The things we do for the glory of God should be done with cheerfulness, with songs of praise and thanksgiving, not with sadness and gloom.

Our God is a tender and merciful Father. Living for Him should not be looked upon as doing something that brings sadness or distress to our heart. We should consider it a pleasure to worship the Lord and to help with His work. God doesn't want His children, for whom such a great pardon has been given, to act as if He is a hard slave driver. He is our best Friend, and when we worship Him, He counts on being with us to bless, comfort and fill our hearts with joy and love. The Lord wants His children to feel comforted while doing His service and to find more pleasure than hardship in His work. He wants those who come to worship Him to carry away with them precious thoughts of His care and love. When we dwell on His goodness we will be happy in our daily life and have the grace to be honest and faithful in all things.

(23) WHAT SHOULD BE THE THEME OF OUR THOUGHTS AND CONVERSATIONS?

____

____

____

Psalms 50:23

Our thoughts should be centered around the cross and His death there for us. This should be the main theme on our minds, the center of what we talk about, and our most joyful feeling. We should keep in our thoughts every blessing we receive from God. When we come to understand His great love we should be willing to trust everything in the hands that were nailed to the cross for us.

(24) WHAT SHOULD ALWAYS BE ON OUR LIPS?

____

____

____

Isaiah 51:3

Our soul may be raised nearer to heaven when we praise Him. God is worshiped with song and music in the courts of heaven above, and as we give Him our thanks we are imitating the worship of the heavenly angels. Let us, in the spirit of reverent joy, come before our Creator with "thanksgiving and the voice of melody."

I am thankful to God for the privilege of prayer. I accept His invitation to come "boldly before His throne of grace" so that I may obtain the grace and the mercy He promises.

Circle: Yes No Undecided

I am realizing how prayer is the breath of my spiritual life. It is my desire to live in constant connection with Him and experience His abiding peace.

Circle: Yes No Undecided

It is my desire to not just pray for others but to show God's love for them by allowing Him to use me to help fulfill their needs.

Circle: Yes No Undecided

I now realize that prayer isn't just for asking and receiving from God. It is my goal to make it a time of thanksgiving and praise to Him for the countless blessings He graciously gives.

Circle: Yes No Undecided

Study notes: ______________________________

Over Coming Doubt

Lesson 12

(1) WHAT RESPONSE DID JESUS GIVE TO THOSE WHO WERE SKEPTICAL OF HIS DIVINITY?

____

____

____

Matthew 12:39

Many people, especially those who are new to the Christian life, are sometimes troubled with thoughts of doubt. There are many things in the Bible which they cannot explain, or even understand. Satan uses these to try to do away with their faith in the Scriptures and convince them they are not a revelation from God. They ask, "How can I know the right way? If the Bible is the sure Word of God, how can I become free from these doubts and questions?"

God never asks us to believe of His existence without giving enough evidence to base our faith upon. His character and the truthfulness of His Word are all based on testimony that is reasonable and plentiful. But still God has never taken away the possibility for doubt. Our faith must rest on evidence, not on display. Those who wish to doubt will have their chance, while those who desire to know truth will find plenty of evidence to base their faith on.

(2) WHY CAN'T MAN UNDERSTAND THE WAYS OF GOD?

____

____

____

Isaiah 55:8,9

It is not possible for our limited minds to know fully the character or the works of God who is the Unlimited One. To the smartest and most educated mind God will always remain hidden in mystery. "Canst thou by searching find out God? Canst thou find out the Almighty unto perfection? It is as high as heaven; what canst thou do? Deeper than hell; what canst thou know?" Job 11:7, 8.

The apostle Paul said, "O the depth of the riches both of the wisdom and knowledge of God! How unsearchable are His judgments, and His ways past finding out!" Romans 11:33. But though "clouds and darkness are round about Him," "righteousness and judgment are the habitation of His throne." Psalm 97:2. We can understand the way He deals with us and the motives by which He moves, enough to see the endless love and mercy that are part of His unlimited power. He lets us understand as much of His ways that is for our good to know; and beyond this, we must still trust the hand that is almighty and the heart that is full of love.

(3) WHEN WE FAIL TO UNDERSTAND SCRIPTURE WHAT CAUTION SHOULD WE HEED?

____

____

____

____

____

____

2 Peter 3:16,17

The Word of God is like the character of the Holy One who wrote it: it shows us mysteries that can never be totally understood by our limited minds. Some of these mysteries that are too deep for the human mind to explain, or even to fully understand are: the coming of sin into the world, the first coming of Christ, how we can be born again, Christ's resurrection, and many other subjects presented in the Bible. We do not have any reason to doubt God's Word just because we cannot understand the mysteries of His creative power. In the world we see and touch we are always surrounded with mysteries that we cannot understand. The very simplest form of life is something that the wisest of philosophers are unable to explain. Everywhere are wonders beyond our reach. Since this is true should we be surprised to find that in the spiritual world there are also mysteries that we cannot understand? The problem lies only in how weak and narrow the human mind is. In the Scriptures God has given us plenty of signs to show their godly character. We are not to doubt His Word because we cannot understand all the mysteries of His ruling power.

The apostle Peter says "things hard to be understood, which they that are unlearned and unstable wrest . . . unto their own destruction." Because they don't understand Scripture, many unbelievers use this to argue against the Bible. But what is true is that they have strong proof of it being divinely inspired. If the Bible and what it says about God could all be understood, if His greatness and glory could be comprehended by our limited minds; then, the Bible would not carry the unmistakable mark of coming from Heaven. The very richness and mystery of the topics that are revealed should bring us to a deeper faith in it as the Word of God.

(4) DOES WISDOM OF THIS WORLD GIVE UNDERSTANDING OF SCRIPTURE?

____

____

____

____

1 Corinthians 2:14

The Bible reveals truth to the reader by providing a simple and a perfect fit to the needs and desires of our heart. This has amazed and charmed the smartest minds, but at the same time it shows the humble and unlearned the way to be saved. And yet these truths, told in a simple manner, are at the same time subjects so great, so far-reaching, so far beyond the power of our human minds to understand, that we can accept them only because God has said it is so. In this way God's plan to save us is shown. These truths are revealed so that every one of us may see the steps we should take in admission and sorrow for sin. They show the faith we must have in Jesus. By knowing these steps we may be saved in God's way. Underneath these truths that are so easily understood lie secret things that are hiding His glory. These secret things are overpowering to our mind as we study, but still fill us with respect and faith when we are really looking for truth. The more we search the Bible, the deeper is our belief that it is the Word of the living God. Our human thoughts begin to understand these great truths that heaven has revealed.

To say that we cannot fully understand the great truths of the Bible is only to admit that our limited minds are not able to grasp the unlimited. It is just saying that man, with his limited human knowledge, cannot fully understand the plan of God.

(5) WHAT ARE WE WARNED TO NOT LET ENTER OUR HEARTS?

____

____

Hebrews 3:12

The doubter and the unbelievers deny God's Word because they cannot grasp all its secrets. And all who claim to believe the Bible are not free from this same danger. The apostle warns us in the above verse about this. It is good to study closely the things the Bible teaches and to search into "the deep things of God" as far as they are shown to us in Scripture. 1 Corinthians 2:10. Satan will do his best to cause us to question things. Some people let pride get involved when trying to consider Bible truth. They feel impatient and defeated if they cannot explain every part of the Bible the way they would like to. It is too humiliating for them to admit that they do not understand the inspired words of God. They are unwilling to wait patiently until God sees fit to show the truth to them. They feel that their human wisdom alone is enough for them to be able to understand the Scriptures, and because of this they are denying its power. It is true that many of the theories and doctrines that are popular to believe are supposed to have come from the Bible but are not based on what it teaches. They even go against inspiration. These things have been a cause of doubt and confusion to many minds. This doubt cannot be blamed on God's Word, but rather on man's changing of it.

(6) WHY WILL WE NEVER BE ABLE TO FULLY UNDERSTAND GOD?

____

____

____

____

Deuteronomy 29:29

If it were possible for us as created beings to be able to fully understand God and everything He does; then, once we reached that point, there would be no more truth for us to discover. There would be nothing else to learn, and no further need for our mind and heart to mature. God would no longer be exalted, and if we could reach the limit of learning and fulfillment, we would no longer improve. We should thank God that it is not that way. God is without limit, in Him are "all the treasures of wisdom and knowledge." Colossians 2:3. Throughout eternity we will always be searching, always learning, and still we will never find all the treasures of His wisdom, His goodness, and His power.

(7) WHERE ONLY CAN GODLY WISDOM BE OBTAINED?

1 Corinthians 2:12

In this life the truths of His word shall always be unfolding to His people. There is only one way in which this wisdom can be obtained. We can gain an understanding of God's Word only by the same source the Word was given - by the Holy Spirit showing it to us. "The things of God knoweth no man, but the Spirit of God;" "the Spirit searcheth all things, yea, the deep things of God."

(8) WHAT WILL WE FIND WHEN WE ALLOW THE HOLY SPIRIT TO GUIDE US AS WE STUDY?

John 16:13

God wants us to use our ability to think, and as we study the Bible it will strengthen and lift up our minds like nothing else can. Yet we should remember that our reasoning is affected by our human weakness and feebleness. We should always be pleading with the Holy Spirit to open our minds to the Scriptures. We have to have the simple faith of a child and be ready to learn or we will not understand even the plainest truths. We should be humbled because we sense the power and wisdom of God, and because we can't understand His greatness. We should open His Word in the same way we would enter His presence, with holy reverence, and our reason must admit that God's power is greater then our own. When we come to the Bible, our heart and mind must bow to the great I AM.

(9) WHO IS OUR SOURCE OF WISDOM?

James 1:5

There are many things that appear to be difficult or unclear, but God will make plain and simple to those who look for understanding with His help. But without the help of the Holy Spirit we will always be in danger of coming to the wrong understanding or losing interest in the scriptures altogether. Many times the Bible is read and nothing is gained; in fact, it ends with negative results. Doubt grows stronger when the Word of God is opened without respect and without prayer. If our thoughts and our love are not fixed upon God, or in tune with His will, our mind will be clouded with doubts. The enemy takes control of the thoughts and he tries to lead us to an understanding of God's Word that is not true. If we are not trying to be in tune with God in both the words we say and the things we do, then no matter how smart we are we will likely misunderstand the Scriptures. When someone is in that condition it is not safe to trust what they say about the Bible. Those who look in the Scriptures to find things that they think are wrong, are not being guided by the Holy Spirit. Since they don't see clearly they will see many reasons for doubt and unbelief in things that are really plain and simple.

(10) IF WE BLATANTLY CONTINUE IN KNOWN SIN HOW DOES THIS AFFECT OUR RELATIONSHIP WITH GOD?

Isaiah 59:2

Many people try hard to hide it, but in most cases the love of sin is the real reason they have doubts and have questions about spiritual things. The direction given in God's Word is not welcomed by the proud, sin-loving heart who is not willing to obey what it says but are ready to doubt its authority. In order for us to find truth, we really must want to know the truth and be willing in our heart to obey it. All who come to study the Bible in this way will find more than enough evidence that it is God's word. When they look they will gain an understanding of its truths that will make them wise unto salvation.

(11) WHAT DOES GOD REQUIRE OF US BEFORE REVEALING NEW LIGHT?

____

____

____

John 7:17

Instead of questioning and finding fault about the things you don't understand, live according to the light that already shines upon you, and then you will receive greater light. By the grace of Christ, do every thing that you understand to be right and then you will be able to understand and do those things about which you are now in doubt.

The proof that comes from experience is there for all to have from the most highly educated to the least educated. God invites us to prove for ourselves how real His Word is and see the truth of His promises. He invites us to "taste and see that the Lord is good." Psalm 34:8. Instead of depending on what someone else tells us, we are to taste for ourselves. He tells us, "Ask, and ye shall receive." John 16:24. His promises will happen as He says. They have never failed and they never can fail. As we draw near to Jesus and praise Him in the fullness of His love, our doubt and darkness will disappear in the light of His presence.

(12) AS OUR RELATIONSHIP WITH JESUS DEVELOPS WHAT WILL BE OUR TESTIMONTY?

____

____

____

____

Colossians 1:13

____

____

____

James 1:18

The apostle Paul says that God "hath delivered us from the power of darkness," and everyone who has passed from death unto life is able to "set to his seal that God is true." Colossians.1:13, John 3:33. He can say, "I needed help and I found it in Jesus. Everything I needed was given and the hunger of my soul was satisfied. Now the Bible reveals Jesus Christ to me. Do you ask why I believe in Jesus? Because He is to me a Holy Saviour. Why do I believe the Bible? Because I have found it to be the voice of God speaking to my soul." We can show others that God's Word is true and that Jesus is the Son of God by keeping it in our hearts. We know that we are not following cleverly devised stories.

(13) WHEN WE FOLLOW THE LIGHT THAT WE HAVE BEEN GIVEN, WHAT BENEFITS WILL BE SEEN?

____

____

____

Proverbs 4:18,19

Peter encourages his brethren to "grow in grace, and in the knowledge of our Lord and Saviour Jesus Christ." When the people of God are growing in grace, they will always be getting a clearer understanding of His Word. They will sense new light and beauty in its holy truths. This has been true in the history of the church through all ages, and it will be the same way to the end.

(14) WHAT PROMISE ARE WE GIVEN FOR THE FUTRUE AS WE CONTINUE IN JESUS?

____

____

____

1 Corinthians 13:12

By faith we may look to the future and accept the promise of God that He will help us to grow in wisdom and cause our human strength to come together with His. Every power of our soul will be brought into touch with the Source of light. We may give praise that everything that has troubled us is under the power of God and He will make it clear to us. For things that we find hard to understand we will find an answer, and where our limited minds find only confusion and broken purposes, we shall see the most perfect and beautiful harmony.

I realize that in the final days of earth's history many will be skeptical of God. I choose to base my faith on the evidences He has provided and believe in Him.

Circle: Yes No Undecided

It is comforting to me to know that God's wisdom cannot be understood by any man. I can place my life in His hands knowing He is in control of all things.

Circle: Yes No Undecided

I realize that even though I cannot understand all that the Bible says about God, this is even more proof of His greatness. It is evident that the Bible is inspired by Him.

Circle: Yes No Undecided

I choose to put away all doubts that the Tempter plants in my mind concerning God and His Word. I choose to follow the light as God sees fit to reveal it to me.

Circle: Yes No Undecided

Study notes: _______________

Happiness in Jesus

Lesson 13

(1) AS CHRISTIANS, WHO ARE WE TO TELL OF CHRIST'S LOVE?

____

____

John 17:18

As children of God it is our privilege to show the rest of the world what Jesus is like; we should show the goodness and mercy of the Lord. Just as Jesus has shown us the true character of the Father, we are to show what Jesus is like to a world that does not know His tender, pitying love.

(2) WHEN WE ACCEPT THE TITLE OF CHRISTIAN, WHAT IS OUR ROLE TO FULFILL?

____

____

____

____

2 Corinthians 3:2,3

In every one of His children, Jesus sends a letter to the world. If you are Christ's follower, He sends you as a letter to your family, your town, and the street where you live. Jesus desires to speak through you to the hearts of those who do not know Him. Perhaps they do not read the Bible, or do not hear the voice that speaks to them in its pages. They do not see the love of God through the things He does. But if you are a true example of Jesus, it may be that through you they will be led to understand what His goodness is like and be won to love and serve Him.

(3) WHAT WONDERFUL MESSAGE OF HOPE DO CHRISTIANS HAVE THE PRIVILEGE OF SHARING?

____
____
____
____
____

John 17:23

Christians are to be the bearers of light on their way to heaven. They are to reflect to the world the light shining upon them from Christ. Their life should be such that through them others will get the right picture of Christ and His service. Isaiah 12:4.

If we show what Jesus is like to others, we will show that living for Him is as desirable as it really is. Christians who look on the gloomy and sad side of things, the ones who are always grumbling and complaining, are giving the wrong picture to others of what God is like and what the Christian life is. They give others the idea that God is not pleased to have His children happy, and by doing this they are not showing who our loving heavenly Father is.

(4) AS CHRISTIANS WHAT TYPE OF ATTITUDE SHOULD WE HAVE?

____
____
____

Philippians 4:11

Satan is thrilled when he can lead the children of God to stop believing and become unhappy. He is delighted when he sees us distrusting God and doubting that God is willing or that He even has the power to save us. He loves to make us think that the Lord will harm us by the way He rules. It is the goal of Satan to make others believe that the Lord does not show enough care nor have pity on us. Satan lies and fills our minds with wrong ideas about God. Instead of thinking about our heavenly Father as we should, too much of the time we think about the lies of Satan. When we do this we fail to honor God by our complaining and lack of trust. Satan is always trying to make our spiritual lives gloomy. He wants the Christain life to look difficult to others; he desires it to appear to be a lot of work. If we as Christians show this in our own lives, through our unbelief, we are telling the same lies as Satan.

(5) WHAT ATTITUDE SHOULD WE HAVE AS WE FACE THE DIFFICULTIES OF LIFE?

____
____
____
____

2 Corinthians 12:9,10

Many people, as they go through life, are always thinking about their mistakes and the times they have failed and been disappointed. When we think about these things our hearts become filled with sorrow and hope is weakened.

Life is like walking through a rose garden. As you pass through it's experiences you can choose to focus on the briers and thorns, or the beauty of the flowers. The briers and thorns will only hurt you and cause suffering. If you only gather these things and point them out to others; aren't you keeping those around you from walking in the path of life? Aren't you taking away from the goodness of God? It is not wise to gather together all the unpleasant memories of your past life, all of the bad you have done and the disappointments you have had. It is not good to keep repeating them and mourning over them until you are overwhelmed with discouragement. If you choose this path you will be depressed and filled with darkness. It will cause the light of God to be shut out from your soul and you will then cast a shadow upon the pathway of others.

Let us as thankful Christians pass through the experiences of life dwelling on the beauty of the flowers. These are the bright spots in our lives and the precious times when our hearts throbbed with joy in response to the Spirit of God.

When you look back through the experiences of your life do you find some pleasant times? Are God's promises, like the sweet smelling flowers, growing on both sides of your path? Will you let their beauty and sweetness fill your heart with joy?

(6) WHAT PICTURE OF GOD SHOULD THE CHRISTIAN'S LIFE PORTRAY?

____

____

____

____

____

____

Isaiah 12:4,5

Thank God for the bright pictures which He has given to us. Let us consider all these blessed assurances of His love and always keep them in mind. The Son of God left His Father's throne and clothed His divinity with humanity so that He could come and rescue us from the power of Satan. Christ's victory opened heaven so the Glory of the Lord could be seen. The fallen race was uplifted from the pit of ruin into which sin had caused it to fall, and brought again into touch with the eternal God. And, after having endured the divine test through faith in our Redeemer, we are clothed in the righteousness of Christ and then exalted to His throne. All these are the pictures that God wants us to keep in our minds and share with others.

(7) HOW DID GOD PROVE HIS LOVE FOR US BEYOND ANY DOUBT?

____

____

____

Romans 8:32

When we doubt God's love and distrust His promises we dishonor Him and grieve His Holy Spirit. How would a mother feel if her children were constantly complaining that she did not want what is best for them when her whole life's effort had been to do all she could to give them comfort? If they should doubt her love for them, it would break her heart. How would any parents feel to be treated this way by their children? And what does our heavenly Father think about us when we distrust His love, the love which led Him to give His only begotten Son that we might have life? And yet how many of us by our actions, if not our words, are saying, "The Lord does not mean these promises for me. Perhaps He loves others, but He does not love me."

(8) WHY SHOULD WE NOT SHARE DOUBT AND DISCOURAGEMENT WITH OTHERS?

____

____

____

____

Romans 14:13

When we distrust the Lord it is only harming our own souls because every word of doubt we speak is inviting Satan to tempt us. Distrust strengthens in us the tendency to doubt, and it grieves and draws the ministering angels away from us. When Satan tempts us, we should not breathe a word of doubt or darkness. If we choose to open the door to his suggestions, our minds will be filled with distrust and rebellious questions. If we talk out our feelings, every doubt we express not only has an effect on us, but it is a seed that will grow and cause doubt in the lives of others. It may be impossible to make up for the effect of our words on them. We ourselves may be able to recover from the moment of temptation and from the trap of Satan, but others who have been swayed by our influence may not be able to escape from the unbelief we have planted in them. This is why it is so important that we speak only those things that will give spiritual strength and life!

(9) WHY IS IT IMPORTANT TO RIGHTLY REPRESENT CHRIST BY OUR WORDS?

____

____

Romans 14:7

____

____

____

____

1 Corinthians 8:12

Angels are listening to hear what you are telling the world about your heavenly Master. When you speak let it be about Jesus who lives to represent us before the Father. When you take the hand of a friend, let praise to God be on your lips and in your heart. This will attract his thoughts to Jesus.

(10) WHAT ADVISE DOES THE BIBLE GIVE US TO HANDLE DOUBT AND DISCOURAGMENT?

____

____

____

____

Philipians 2:14

Everyone has trials, sorrows hard to bear, and temptations hard to resist. Do not tell your troubles to your fellow mortals, but carry everything to God in prayer. Make it a rule never to speak one word of doubt or discouragement. You can do much to brighten the lives of others and strengthen their efforts by words of hope and blessed comfort.

There are many brave souls being attacked by temptation. They are almost ready to give up in the battle with self and with the powers of evil. Do not discourage those that are going through these hard struggles. Cheer them up with brave, hopeful words that will help them along the road they are traveling. In this way the light of Christ may shine from you. "None of us liveth to himself." Romans 14:7. By our influence others may be encouraged and strengthened, or they may be discouraged and pushed away from Christ and the truth.

(11) IN WHOSE PRESENCE IS THE FULLNESS OF JOY AND PLEASURE FOUND?

____

____

____

Psalms 16:11

There are many who have a false idea about the life and character of Christ. They think that He was without warmth and was not pleasant; that He was hard, severe, and without joy. In many cases their whole religious experience is affected by these gloomy views.

It is often said that Jesus wept, but that He was never known to smile. Our Saviour was indeed a "Man of Sorrows," and "acquainted with grief." This was because He opened His heart to all the troubles of men. But though His life was unselfish and shadowed with pain and care, His spirit was not crushed. His appearance did not wear an expression of sadness and gloom, but instead one of peaceful calmness. His heart was a source of life, and wherever He went He carried rest, peace, joy and gladness.

Our Saviour was deeply serious and very earnest, but never gloomy or unhappy. The life of those who imitate Him will be full of earnest purpose and they will have a deep sense of personal responsibility. Lightness of purpose will be held back, and there will be no rough pleasure seeking and no rude joking. But instead, the faith of Jesus gives peace like a river. It does not hold back the light of joy; it does not restrain cheerfulness nor cloud the sunny, smiling face. Christ came not to be ministered unto but to minister and when His love reigns in our heart, we will follow His example.

(12) WHAT SHOULD WE DO WHEN OTHERS OFFEND US?

____

____

____

Ephesians 4:32

____

____

____

Proverbs 19:11

If we are always thinking about the unkind and unfair things that others do we will find it impossible to love them as Christ has loved us. But, if our thoughts are about the wonderful love and mercy that Christ has for us, we will show the same spirit and it will flow out to others. We should love and respect one another in spite of the faults and flaws that we cannot help seeing. It should be our goal to be humble and not to trust ourselves. We should be patient and tender when it comes to the faults of others. This will take away all the selfishness and give us a large heart that will help us to be generous.

(13) WHY SHOULD WE TELL OUR PROBLEMS ONLY TO GOD?

____

____

____

Hebrews 13:6

The psalmist says, "Trust in the Lord, and do good; so shalt thou dwell in the land, and verily thou shalt be fed." Psalm 37:3. Each day has its burdens and its cares. Things happen that we don't understand and when we meet with others we should avoid telling them our difficulties and trials. When we share troubles it takes away our peace of mind. We are allowing fears to come in and the result is stress and anxiety. Because of all this it would appear to others that we don't have a loving Saviour who has love and mercy for us, who is ready to hear all our prayers and to be there to help us in time of need.

(14) WILL GOD DESERT US IN ANY SITUATION?

____

____

____

Hebrews 13:5

Some people are always full of fear and borrowed trouble. Every day they are surrounded with tokens of God's love and are enjoying the fruit that comes from His hand, yet they overlook the blessings that are always present. Their minds are always thinking about something bad that they fear might happen; or some difficulty may really exist which, though small, blinds their eyes to the many things that should receive their thanks. The hard times they go through keeps them from peace. The gloom that results separates them from God instead of bringing them to Him, the only source of help.

Does it do us any good to be unbelieving like this? Why should we be ungrateful and distrusting? Jesus is our friend and all of heaven is interested in what happens to us. We should not allow the things we don't understand and the cares of everyday life to worry us and cause us to be gloomy. If we do this we will always have something to bother and disturb us. We should not dwell on things that only cause worry and wear us down since this worry will not help us to get though our trials.

(15) WHAT WILL THE LORD DO FOR US IF WE TRUST AND FOLLOW HIM?

Proverbs 3:5,6

You may have troubles in your business, your prospects may grow darker and darker, and you may be threatened with loss. If this happens do not become discouraged; cast your cares upon God and remain calm and cheerful. Pray for wisdom to manage your affairs wisely, to keep from loss and disaster. Do all you can on your part to bring about favorable results. Jesus has promised His help, but not unless we put forth the effort. When you have relied on the Lord and you have done all you can, then accept the result cheerfully.

(16) AS WE FACE TRIALS WHAT ENCOURAGEMENT DOES GOD GIVE US?

John 16:33

It is not the will of God that His people should be weighed down with the cares of this world. But our Lord does not deceive us. He does not say to us, "Do not fear; there are no dangers in your path." He knows there are trials and dangers, and is honest about it. He does not suggest that His people should be taken out of a world of sin and evil, but He points them to a never-failing refuge.

(17) WHAT PROMISE CAN WE CLAIM CONCERNING OUR DAILY NEEDS?

Matthew 6:33

In His Sermon on the Mount in Matthew chapter five, Christ taught His disciples precious lessons about the need of trusting in God. These lessons were given to encourage the children of God through all ages, and they have come down to our time full of instruction and comfort. The Saviour pointed His followers to the birds of the air, who sing their carols of praise free from care for, "they sow not, neither do they reap." And yet the great Father provides for their needs. The Saviour asks, "Are ye not much better than they?" The great Provider for man and beast opens His hand and supplies all His creatures' needs. He even notices the birds of the air. He does not drop the food into their bills, but He makes available the things they need. They have to gather the grains He has scattered for them. They must prepare the material for their little nests and feed their young. It is true "your heavenly Father feedeth them" and "are ye not much better than they?" Aren't you, as intelligent, spiritual worshipers of more value than the birds of the air? Won't the Author of our being, the Preserver of our life, the One who formed us in His own divine image, provide for our needs if we will only trust in Him?

(18) WHAT DOES CHRIST ASK US TO CONSIDER AS ASSURANCE OF HIS LOVING AND CARE?

Matthew 6:28-30

Christ pointed His disciples to the flowers of the field, growing in rich abundance and glowing in the simple beauty which the heavenly Father had given them, as a way to show His love to man. He said, "Consider the lilies of the field, how they grow." These natural flowers, simple and full of beauty, go beyond the glory of Solomon. The most gorgeous clothing made with the skill of art cannot compare with the natural grace and shining beauty of the flowers of God's creation. If God, the divine Artist, gives to the simple flowers that die in a day their delicate and varied colors, how much greater care will He have for those who are created in His own image? With this lesson Jesus is scolding the faithless heart that has fearful thoughts and is uncertain and full of doubt. The Lord wants to have all His sons and daughters happy, peaceful, and obedient, so He has given us this wonderful promise.

(19) WHAT WILL JESUS GIVE TO THOSE THAT SERVE HIM?

____

____

John 14:27

When someone goes out of his way to search for happiness for selfish reasons, the results will be unbalanced, changeable, and passing. When he searches in this way the heart is filled with loneliness and sorrow. On the other hand there is joy, happiness, and peace in the service of God. The Christian is not left to walk in uncertain paths; he is not left with worthless regrets and failures. Even if we do not have the pleasures of this life we may still be joyful in looking to the life beyond.

(20) BY TRUSTING COMPLETELY IN CHRIST WHAT PROMISE OF COMFORT IS OURS?

____

____

____

Matthew 28:20

Even here on earth Christians may have the joy that comes from being close to Christ. They may have the light of His love, and the constant comfort of His presence. Every step in life may bring us closer to Jesus, give us a deeper experience of His love, and may bring us one step nearer to the blessed home of peace. Then let's not throw away our trust, but have even stronger belief. "Hitherto hath the Lord helped us," and He will help us to the end. 1 Samuel 7:12.

(21) WHY SHOULD WE KEEP THE BLESSINGS GOD HAS GIVEN US FRESH IN OUR MINDS?

____

____

____

____

____

Deuteronomy 4:9

Let us look to the mighty pillars God has given us as reminders of what He has done to comfort and to save us from the hand of the destroyer. Let us keep fresh in our memory all the tender mercies that God has shown us: the tears He has wiped away, the pains taken away, the worry removed, the fears taken away; the things we wanted He supplied, the blessings He has given. Remembering these things will give us strength for all that is before us through the rest of our journey.

(22) WHAT ARE WE PROMISED AS WE FACE THE TRIALS AND TRIBULATIONS THAT WE MUST BEAR?

____

____

____

____

1Peter 5:10

____

____

____

Job 23:10

We may look back on past trials as well as on what is to come, and say, "Hitherto hath the Lord helped us." "As thy days, so shall thy strength be." Deuteronomy 33:25. The trial will not be greater than the strength that will be given to us to bear it. Then let us do our work wherever we find it and believe that whatever trial may come, God will provide the strength needed.

(23) WHAT CAN WE HAVE JOY IN KNOWING?

____

____

____

____

____

Romans 8:28

(24) WHAT WONDERFUL WORDS CAN WE LOOK FORWARD TO HEARING AS OVERCOMERS?

____

____

____

____

Matthew 25:34

When the time is right the gates of heaven will be thrown open to let in God's children, and from the lips of the King of glory the blessing in the verse above will fall on their ears like sweet music. Then those who are saved will be welcomed to the home that Jesus has prepared for them. They will not be in the company of the evil ones of this earth: the liars, the worshiper of idols, the impure, and the unbelieving. They will be with those who have overcome Satan and through divine grace have formed perfect characters. Every sinful tendency and every imperfection that bothers them here has been removed by the blood of Christ. The excellence and brightness of His glory is given to them that far exceeds the brightness of the sun. The moral beauty which is the perfection of His character will shine through them in worth far exceeding this outward brightness. They are without any faults before the great white throne, sharing the honor and the privileges of the angels.

(25) AS WE FACE ETERNITY WHAT IMPORTANT QUESTION SHOULD WE BE ASKING OURSELVES?

____

____

____

____

Matthew 16:26

In view of the glorious inheritance that may be ours, is there anything this world has that is worth losing our soul over? We may be poor, yet we possess a wealth and honor that the world could never give. The soul redeemed and cleansed from sin, with all its good powers dedicated to the service of God, is of great value. There is joy in heaven in the presence of God and the holy angels over one soul redeemed, a joy that is expressed in songs of holy triumph.

I give my whole heart to Jesus and accept the magnificent grace He offers me. I accept the honor of bearing the name "Christian."

Circle: Yes No Undecided

It is my desire to be a happy Christian and to reveal the joy, peace, and happiness that comes from abiding in Him to others.

Circle: Yes No Undecided

I thank God for revealing the steps for me to come to Him in His Word. As I have completed this lesson series I have felt the Holy Spirit leading me into a closer walk with Christ.

Circle: Yes No Undecided

I am interested in receiving other Bible based study courses that are available. I want to better understand God's plan for my life.

Circle: Yes No Undecided

The words of your answer may vary according to the translation of the Bible you use, but the overall meaning should remain the same.

Lesson 1

(1) He provides our food and satisfies our desires.
(2) God is love.
(3) Pardons iniquity, forgiving of transgressions, delights in mercy.
(4) To be fearful of Him.
(5) No man hath seen God at any time.
(6) The Son will reveal Him.
(7) To preach the gospel, to heal the brokenhearted, to preach deliverance, to give sight to the blind, to set at liberty the bruised.
(8) In the flesh...with grace and truth.
(9) Despised and rejected, not esteemed but considered stricken, smitten of God, and afflicted. Wounded for our transgressions, bruised for our iniquities.
(10) My God, My God, why have You forsaken Me.
(11) To reconcile the world unto Himself.
(12) I lay down my life that I might take it again. No man taketh it I lay it down Myself.
(13) He is not ashamed to call us brethren.
(14) We are called the children of God.

Lesson 2

(1) Wisdom and good understanding.
(2) They were afraid because of their nakedness.
(3) To cry for the rocks and mountains to fall on them to hide from His face and wrath.
(4) Not one.
(5) Be born again.
(6) They are spiritually understood.
(7) We, like Paul, are sold under sin.
(8) The Lamb of God who taketh away the sins of the world.
(9) Jesus is the way.
(10) No man cometh unto the Father but by Me.
(11) The good shepherd giveth His life for the sheep.

Lesson 3

(1) Repent.
(2) The True Light.
(3) (a) Have mercy upon me, cleanse me from sin, I acknowledge my transgression.
(b) Create in me a clean heart and renew a right spirit within me.
(4) Blessed in he whose transgression is forgiven.
(5) Come unto me (Christ) and learn of me.
(6) Our Saviour gives repentance.
(7) All men (every person.)
(8) Let him who is thirsty come, let him take the water of life freely.
(9) We are unclean, our righteousness are as filthy rags.
(10) Lost His strength.
(11) Sin revived and I died.
(12) Pride.
(13) God be merciful to me a sinner.
(14) Without Me (Christ) ye can do nothing.
(15) In his sin he shall die.
(16) Christ left an example that we should follow His steps.
(17) A man's heart deviseth his steps.
(18) Shall be holden with the cords of his sins.
(19) Now is the accepted time, now it the day of salvation.
(20) The Lord looketh on the heart.
(21) Peace with all men, and holiness.
(22) Reconciling the world to Himself.
(23) Came to save sinners.
(24) He to whom He forgave most.

Lesson 4

(1) Confess and forsake them.
(2) (a) God
(b) One to another.
(3) Broken heart and contrite (sorrow for sin) spirit.
(4) Confess that (specific thing) he hath sinned.
(5) Asked for a king.
(6) Cease to do evil.

(7) Restore - give that which was taken.
(8) (a) The man said the woman.
(b) The woman said the serpent.
(9) A sinner.
(10) "I" five times.
(11) He is faithful and just to forgive us our sins and to cleanse us from all unrighteousness.

Lesson 5

(1) Search with all your heart.
(2) Dead in trespasses and sin.
(3) Come now let us reason together.
(4) Forsake all for Christ.
(5) We are saved through faith not of ourselves, it is the gift of God.
(6) Laid on Him the iniquity of us all.
(7) Christ poured out his soul unto death. He was numbered with the transgressors. He bore the sins of many. He made intercession for the transgressors.
(8) Seek first the kingdom of God and His righteousness.
(9) He shall supply all our needs.
(10) Choose this day to serve the Lord.
(11) Not everyone that saith unto me Lord, Lord shall enter the kingdom of heaven.

Lesson 6

(1) There is no peace unto the wicked.
(2) Every one that thirsteth, he with no money.
(3) A new heart will I give you and a new spirit will I put within you.
(4) That we might believe that Jesus is the Son of God and that believing ye might have life through His name.
(5) Believe that He is able to do it.
(6) Not one.
(7) The Father gives good things to those who ask
(8) As ye have received Christ continue to walk in Him.
(9) I will give you rest.
(10) I have blotted out thy transgressions. I have redeemed thee.
(11) Not to condemn the world but that the world through Him might be saved.
(12) With compassion.
(13) Him that cometh I will in no wise cast out.
(14) (a) I will not forget thee.
(b) I will never leave thee nor forsake thee.

Lesson 7

(1) Can't tell where it comes from, and where it goes.
(2) If any man be in Christ he is a new creature.
(3) Love, joy, peace, long-suffering, gentleness, goodness, faith, meekness, temperance.
(4) Restore (repay.)
(5) Because He first loved us.
(6) Keep (obey) his commandments.
(7) He that saith I know Him and keepeth not His commandments is a liar and the truth is not in Him.
(8) Put my laws into their hearts and their minds.
(9) Ye shall know them by their fruits.
(10) Faith and works.
(11) Christ left us an example that we should follow in His steps.
(12) By the righteousness of God.
(13) Redemption and forgiveness of sins.
(14) We may be partakers of the divine nature and escape corruption.
(15) I live by faith of the Son of God.
(16) The devils also believe and tremble.
(17) He which has begun a good work in you will perform it until the day of Jesus Christ.
(18) (a) If any man sin we have an advocate.
(b) He is faithful and just to forgive us our sins and cleanse us from all unrighteousness.
(19) All our righteousness are as filthy rags.

Lesson 8

(1) By the sincere milk of the Word.
(2) Things of the Spirit of God...these are spiritually discerned.

(3) (a) God is the Sun and Shield.
(b) I (the Lord) will be as the dew unto Israel.

(4) Abide in Him.

(5) Looking unto Jesus the Author and Finisher of our faith.

(6) As ye have received Christ so walk in Him.

(7) Those that seek Me early shall find Me.

(8) (a) Keep our minds stayed on Thee and trust Thee.
(b) By beholding the glory of the Lord we are changed into the same image.

(9) I will give you rest.

(10) Do not fret because of him who prospers by wickedness.

(11) He that hath the Son hath life.

(12) When the righteous turneth away...in his sin shall he die.

(13) Neither shall any man pluck them out of My hand.

(14) When ye search for Me with all your heart.

(15) Elias (Elijah) was a man subject to like passions as we are.

(16) (a) I am with you alway, even unto the end of the world
(b) The Holy Ghost...will teach you all things.

(17) The Father shall give you the Comforter that He may abide with you for ever.

(18) Neither pray I for these alone, but for them also which shall believe on Me through their word.

(19) Grow up into Him in all things.

Lesson 9

(1) Love one another as I have loved you.

(2) Minister and give His life a ransom for many.

(3) Like John say, "Behold the Lamb of God which taketh away the sin of the world."

(4) Liberal soul shall be made fat (prosper.) He that watereth shall be watered (blessed) himself.

(5) Though He was rich yet for our sakes He became poor.

(6) God works in you to will and do of His good pleasure.

(7) Thy light shall rise, He will guide thee, satisfy thy soul in drought, and make fat thy bones.

(8) Look and continue in the perfect law of liberty. Be a doer of the work.

(9) Go ye therefore and teach all nations baptizing them.

(10) Let every man (person) where he (or she) is called abide with God.

(11) Shall be taken away even that which he hath.

(12) Doing service as to the Lord, and not to men.

(13) Whatsoever ye do, do it heartily as to the Lord, and not unto men.

(14) He which soweth bountifully shall also reap bountifully.

Lesson 10

(1) The heavens declare the glory of God and the firmament sheweth His handiwork.

(2) Be still.

(3) The very hairs of your head are numbered.

(4) All things work together for good to them that love God.

(5) Revealed them to us by His Spirit.

(6) He loveth righteousness and judgment...the earth is full of the goodness of the Lord.

(7) Written for our learning, that we through patience and comfort of the scriptures might have hope.

(8) Eternal life and the testimony of Me (Christ.)

(9) Because the words that I speak unto you they are spirit and they are life.

(10) Jesus Christ and Him crucified.

(11) Whatsoever things are true, honest, just, pure, lovely, and things of good report.

(12) To bear the image of the heavenly.

(13) The simple.

(14) Study to shew thyself approved unto God, a workman that needeth not to be ashamed.

(15) Thy Word hidden in the heart.
(16) Precept upon precept, line upon line.
(17) I will answer thee, and shew thee great and mighty things, which thou knowest not.
(18) When He, the Spirit of Truth is come, He will guide you into all truth.

Lesson 11

(1) Pray to Me (God) and I will hearken unto you.
(2) Cast all your care upon Him.
(3) Ought always to pray.
(4) Let us come boldly unto the throne of grace.
(5) Watch and pray.
(6) I will pour water upon him that is thirsty.
(7) Ask and it shall be given you.
(8) He that turneth away his ear from hearing the law, even his prayer shall be abomination.
(9) (a) Ask in faith, nothing wavering.
(b) Believe that ye receive.
(10) Ask, and it shall be given you; seek, and ye shall find; knock, and it shall be opened.
(11) As we forgive our debtors.
(12) Continue in prayer.
(13) Pray to thy Father which is in secret and thy Father which is in secret shall reward thee.
(14) Pray without ceasing.
(15) The peace of God, which passeth all understanding shall keep your hearts and minds.
(16) To heal the broken of heart, and bind up their wounds.
(17) In My (Jesus) name.
(18) (a) Visit the fatherless and the widows.
(b) Go ye therefore and teach all nations, baptizing them.
(19) To exhort (earnestly advise or encourage) one another.
(20) Stayed on Thee (the Lord.)
(21) With thanksgiving let your requests be made known to God.
(22) Ye will rejoice in all...wherein the Lord thy God hath blessed thee.
(23) Offering of praise.
(24) Gladness, thanksgiving, and the voice of melody.

Lesson 12

(1) An evil and adulterous generation seeketh after a sign.
(2) For my thoughts are not your thoughts, neither are your ways My ways saith the Lord.
(3) Beware lest ye also, being led away with the error of the wicked, fall from your own steadfastness.
(4) Then natural man receiveth not the things of the Spirit of God.
(5) Unbelief.
(6) Secret things belong unto the Lord.
(7) The Spirit which is God.
(8) All truth.
(9) God, that giveth to all men liberally.
(10) Your iniquities have separated between you and your God.
(11) If any man (person) will do His will he shall know the doctrine.
(12) (a) He delivered us from darkness.
(b) Begat He us with the word of truth.
(13) Shineth more and more unto the perfect day.
(14) For now we see through a glass, darkly; but then face to face.

Lesson 13

(1) The world.
(2) Ye are our epistle (letter) written in our hearts, known and read of all men.
(3) That the world may know that Thou hast sent Me (Christ) and hast loved them, as thou hast loved Me.
(4) Whatsoever state I am; there to be content.
(5) Most gladly therefore will I rather glory in my infirmities.
(6) Declare His doings among the people, make mention that His name is exalted... for he hath done excellent things: that is known in all the earth.
(7) He spared not His own Son, but delivered Him up for us all.

(8) Putting a stumbling block or an occasion to fall in his brothers way.

(9) (a) None of us liveth to himself.
(b) When ye sin so against the brethren, and wound their conscience ye sin against Christ.

(10) Do all things without murmurings and disputings.

(11) In Thy (the Lord's) presence.

(12) (a) Be ye kind one to another, tender-hearted, forgiving one another.
(b) Passover a transgression.

(13) So we may boldly say the Lord is my Helper.

(14) For he hath said, I will never leave thee, nor forsake thee.

(15) He shall direct thy paths.

(16) In Me ye might have peace.

(17) Seek ye first the kingdom of God, and His righteousness; and all these things will be added unto you.

(18) Consider the Lilies of the field.

(19) My peace I give you.

(20) I am with you always, even unto the end of the world.

(21) Lest thou forget the things which thine eyes have seen, and lest they depart from thy heart.

(22) (a) Perfect, stablish, strengthen, and settle you.
(b) When He hath tried me, I shall come forth as gold.

(23) All things work together for good to them that love God, to those who are called according to His purpose.

(24) Come ye, blessed of my Father, inherit the kingdom prepared for you.

(25) For what is a man profited, if he shall gain the whole world and lose his own soul.

Certificate of Excellence

____

has shown excellence in completion of the

Steps To Christ Bible Study Course

This certificate is to acknowledge that the person named above has successfully completed the Steps to Christ Bible Study Course with excellence.

________________	________	<u>God</u>	________________	________
Certified Course Graduate	**Date**	**Witness**	**Certified Course Instructor**	**Date**

Revelation Publications

Phone 501-549-4048
Visa & Mastercard

P.O. Box 700
Tontitown, AR 72770

ROHM@Juno.com
revelationofhymn.com

Ordered By:

Name: ____________________
Address: ____________________
City: ____________________
State: ________ Zip: __________
Phone: _______ - ____________
Email: ____________________

Deliver To:

Name: ____________________
Address: ____________________
City: ____________________
State: ________ Zip: __________
Phone: _______ - ____________
Email: ____________________

Number of Guides	Unit Price	Quantity	Total
1 to 4	Contact an ABC, Christian book store, or other retailer.		
5 to 24	$2.49		
25 to 49	$1.99		
50 to 499	$1.49		
500 and up	Call for pricing		
		Subtotal	
		Ship/Hand	
		Tax 5.6% (Arkansas only)	
		TOTAL	

CREDIT CARD PURCHASE

Expiration Date: ________

PAYMENT BY: ( ) VISA ( ) MasterCard

Credit Card # : ______________________________

Authorized Signature: ______________________________

PAYMENT BY MONEY ORDER OR CREDIT CARD

PRICE GUARANTEE:

Due to our low profit margins and the fluxuation in printing costs the prices are subject to change. We will contact you prior to filling an order at a different rate.

INTERNATIONAL ORDERS

We will ship by the most economical rate and carrier unless you have requested and paid for faster delivery. These book rates may take 3-6 weeks for delivery. If we ship and there is still additional postage expense we will send an invoice with the balance due upon receipt. All prices listed on this form for books and shipping are in U.S. dollars so you must multiply the total cost of your order by the current exchange rate.

SHIPPING AND HANDLING

5 - 25 books = $5.00
25 and over = 15% of subtotal
International = Multiply all the above x 2

In the U.S. we your order will probably arrive much sooner but please allow at least 3 weeks before contacting us.

RETURNS:

If your books are damaged in shipping or defective due to improper manufacturing, you may return them to us and we will gladly replace them.